The Bathroom Sports

ALMANAC

*Compiled by the Lavatorial Staff
of Red-Letter Press:*

Steve Heldt   John Murphy
Jack Kreismer   Geoff Scowcroft
Ellen Fischbein

Cover and Page Design:
Fred and Diane Swartz

RED-LETTER PRESS, INC.

Saddle River, New Jersey

THE BATHROOM SPORTS ALMANAC
Revised and Updated 2000
Copyright ©1997 Red-Letter Press, Inc.
ISBN: 0-940462-61-3
All Rights Reserved
Printed in the United Sates of America

For information address Red-Letter Press, Inc.
P.O. Box 393, Saddle River, N.J. 07458

JANUARY 1st

TODAY'S THOUGHT: "Sports is the toy department of human life." —*Howard Cosell*

HISTORY: On this date in 1902 the granddaddy of college bowl games was born. Michigan blanked Stanford, 49-0, in the inaugural Rose Bowl (then called the East-West Game). Attendance was so sparse that 14 years passed before the second game was played.

QUIZ: Which NHL team plays its home games in an arena named for a former heavyweight boxing champion?

Trivia Timeout
Hall of Famer Stan Musial tallied 475 home runs in his career, but never hit 40 in a season.

QUIZ ANSWER: The Detroit Red Wings play at the Joe Louis Arena.

JANUARY 2nd

TODAY'S THOUGHT: "It isn't hard to be good from time to time in sports. What's tough is being good every day." —*Willie Mays*

HISTORY: On this date in 1965 Joe Namath signed a $400,000 contract with the New York Jets. Broadway Joe quickly adjusted to life in the Big Apple — especially the nightlife.

QUIZ: Name the only undefeated team to win the Super Bowl.

Trivia Timeout
The only team in the NFL to be owned by a city is the Green Bay Packers.

QUIZ ANSWER: The 1972 Miami Dolphins

JANUARY 3rd

TODAY'S THOUGHT: "I wouldn't believe some pro sports owners even if they swore they were lying."
—Edwin Pope, writer

HISTORY: On this date in 1920 Babe Ruth traded in his red socks for Yankee pinstripes. Boston owner Harry Frazee dealt Ruth to New York to the everlasting dismay of Red Sox loyalists.

QUIZ: What player has won the most NBA MVP awards?

Trivia Timeout
Babe Ruth nicknamed his bat "Black Betsy".

QUIZ ANSWER: Kareem Abdul-Jabbar, who won the award six times

JANUARY 4th

TODAY'S THOUGHT: "When I was losing, they called me nuts. When I was winning, they called me eccentric." *—Al McGuire, former basketball coach*

HISTORY: On this date in 1970 the Kansas City Chiefs defeated the Oakland Raiders, 17-7, in the final American Football League championship game.

QUIZ: Who is the only Major League pitcher to have thrown no-hitters in four consecutive seasons?

Trivia Timeout
Roger Bannister, the first person credited with a sub four-minute mile, didn't break this barrier in an official race. Bannister was actually just paced by two runners on that record-shattering day in 1954.

QUIZ ANSWER: Sandy Koufax, 1962-1965

JANUARY 5th

TODAY'S THOUGHT: "Before you win a game, you have to not lose it." —*Chuck Noll*

HISTORY: On this date in 1971 the Harlem Globetrotters lost a game for the first time in over eight years. After 2,495 straight wins, the Globetrotters were no doubt blue when they were edged, 100-99, by the New Jersey Reds.

QUIZ: What three coaches have led two different teams to the Super Bowl?

Trivia Timeout
The first Super Bowl was televised by both CBS and NBC.

QUIZ ANSWER: Don Shula (Colts and Dolphins), Bill Parcells (Giants and Patriots) and Dick Vermeil (Eagles and Rams)

JANUARY 6th

TODAY'S THOUGHT: "Nothing counts in golf like your opponent." —*Milton Berle*

HISTORY: On this date in 1951 Indianapolis and Rochester battled through six overtimes before Indianapolis prevailed, 75-73, in what remains the longest game in NBA history.

QUIZ: The Norris trophy is awarded annually to the NHL's best defensive player. I won it eight consecutive years. Who am I?

Trivia Timeout
Abbott and Costello are the only two members of the Baseball Hall of Fame not affiliated with baseball. This comedy team was honored for its zany "Who's on First?" routine.

QUIZ ANSWER: Bobby Orr of the Boston Bruins

JANUARY 7th

TODAY'S THOUGHT: "Basketball is like war in that the offensive weapons are developed first, and it always takes a while for the defense to catch up."
—*Red Auerbach*

HISTORY: On this date in 1980 the NHL's longest undefeated streak ended at 35 games when Minnesota stopped Philadelphia, 7-1.

QUIZ: What American cyclist has won the famous Tour de France race three times?

Trivia Timeout
Alvin Dark is the only man to catch a touchdown pass from Y.A. Tittle (in college) and to hit a home run off Sandy Koufax.

QUIZ ANSWER: Greg LeMond won the race in 1986, '89 and '90.

JANUARY 8th

TODAY'S THOUGHT: "It doesn't matter what you accomplish in life; the size of your funeral is going to be determined by the weather."
—*Chuck Tanner, former baseball manager*

HISTORY: On this date in 1955 Adolph Rupp's Kentucky Wildcats had their home winning streak snapped by Georgia Tech. Some of the fans in attendance that night hadn't even been born when the 'Cats basketball team began its 129-game run twelve years earlier.

QUIZ: Who is the NFL's all-time leading scorer?

Trivia Timeout
In greyhound racing, if the dog catches the rabbit (because of mechanical failure), it's considered "no race".

QUIZ ANSWER: George Blanda, with 2,002 points

JANUARY 9th

TODAY'S THOUGHT: "Everybody wants to go to heaven, but nobody wants to die." —*Joe Louis*

HISTORY: On this date in 1942 Joe Louis KO'd Buddy Baer in the first round of their heavyweight championship bout. "The Brown Bomber" donated his entire $76,000 purse to the wartime relief effort.

QUIZ: What were Babe Ruth's real first and middle names?

Trivia Timeout

Joe Louis dropped his last name when he began his boxing career. He was born Joseph Louis Barrow.

QUIZ ANSWER: The Babe was born George Herman Ruth.

JANUARY 10th

TODAY'S THOUGHT: "You observe a lot by just watching." —*Yogi Berra*

HISTORY: On this date in 1982 the Cincinnati Bengals iced the AFC championship with a 27-7 win over the San Diego Chargers. More notable than the score were the temperature (nine below zero) and the wind chill (59 below), making this the coldest playoff game on record.

QUIZ: Name the first wild card team to win a Super Bowl.

Trivia Timeout

The home team must have 24 footballs available for an NFL game.

QUIZ ANSWER: The Oakland Raiders beat Philadelphia, 27-10, in Super Bowl XV.

JANUARY 11th

TODAY'S THOUGHT: "It takes one hell of a man to bring all that glass down and that's just what I proclaim to be." —*Darryl Dawkins, former NBA center and backboard smasher*

HISTORY: On this date in 1973 the American League adopted the designated hitter rule — as an experiment. After a three-year trial, the DH became permanent.

QUIZ: What two teams participated in the first World Series played entirely on artificial turf?

Trivia Timeout

Ron Blomberg of the New York Yankees was baseball's first designated hitter. He walked in his first at-bat.

QUIZ ANSWER: The Philadelphia Phillies and the Kansas Royals in 1980

JANUARY 12th

TODAY'S THOUGHT: "Life don't run from nobody. Life runs at people." —*Joe Frazier*

HISTORY: On this date in 1969 the Jets' $400,000 investment in Joe Namath matured as Namath and his teammates shocked the heavily-favored Baltimore Colts, 16-7, in Super Bowl III.

QUIZ: The 1970 AL batting champion had a brother who gained 1,000 yards in the NFL that same year. Can you name these talented siblings?

Trivia Timeout

Figure skating was an event in the Summer Olympics until 1924, when the first Winter Olympics took place.

QUIZ ANSWER: Alex Johnson, who hit .329 for the Angels and brother, Ron, of the New York Giants

JANUARY 13th

TODAY'S THOUGHT: "If you see a defensive team with dirt and mud on their backs, they've had a bad day."
—*John Madden*

HISTORY: On this date in 1982 Henry Aaron and Frank Robinson were elected to the Baseball Hall of Fame.

QUIZ: What Super Bowl MVP of the 60's later became head coach of his team?

Trivia Timeout

Hank and Tommie Aaron hit more home runs than any other brother combination in baseball history, 768. Hank hit 755 while Tommie contributed 13.

QUIZ ANSWER: Bart Starr of the Green Bay Packers, who was MVP in Super Bowls I and II

JANUARY 14th

TODAY'S THOUGHT: "Winning is not everything — but making the effort to win is." —*Vince Lombardi*

HISTORY: On this date in 1968 Green Bay legend Vince Lombardi coached his last game with the Packers, a 33-14 win over the Oakland Raiders in Super Bowl II.

QUIZ: Who was the first player to catch 100 touchdown passes in the NFL?

Trivia Timeout

Tom Watson is the only American golfer to have won five British Opens.

QUIZ ANSWER: Steve Largent of the Seattle Seahawks, who caught exactly 100 touchdown passes during his career

JANUARY 15th

TODAY'S THOUGHT: "It's a lonesome walk to the sidelines, especially when thousands of people are cheering your replacement." —*Fran Tarkenton*

HISTORY: On this date in 1967 the Green Bay Packers beat the Kansas City Chiefs, 35-10, in the first game between champions of the NFL and AFL—or Super Bowl I.

QUIZ: What two kickers hold the record for the longest field goal in history (63 yards)?

Trivia Timeout

Players on the winning team in the first Super Bowl received $15,000. The losers got $7,500.

QUIZ ANSWER: Tom Dempsey and Jason Elam

JANUARY 16th

TODAY'S THOUGHT: "A lot of folks that ain't saying 'ain't', ain't eating." —*Dizzy Dean, on his atrocious grammar*

HISTORY: On this date in 1962 Bob Pettit of the St. Louis Hawks set an NBA All-Star record by grabbing 27 rebounds. Pettit beat out Wilt Chamberlain, who also set an All-Star record with 42 points, for MVP honors.

QUIZ: Who was the youngest coach in NBA history?

Trivia Timeout

The Kansas City Kings selected decathlon gold medalist Bruce Jenner in the seventh round of the 1977 NBA draft.

QUIZ ANSWER: Dave DeBusschere who, at age 24, was a player-coach for the Detroit Pistons

JANUARY 17th

TODAY'S THOUGHT: "If I was governor or senator, I'd be limited to one state." —*Muhammad Ali, on why he declined running for office*

HISTORY: On this date in 1916, the Professional Golfers Association held its first administrative meeting. The PGA Championship made its debut later that year.

QUIZ: Muhammad Ali was heavyweight champion three times during his career. Can you name the boxers that he defeated to earn the title?

Trivia Timeout

Jack Nicklaus acquired his nickname from his high school, the Upper Arlington (Ohio) Golden Bears.

QUIZ ANSWER: Muhammad Ali defeated Sonny Liston in 1964, George Foreman in 1974 and Leon Spinks in 1978.

JANUARY 18th

TODAY'S THOUGHT: "A well paid slave is a slave nonetheless." —*Curt Flood, on baseball's reserve clause*

HISTORY: On this date in 1983 Jim Thorpe's name was cleared by the International Olympic Committee. Thorpe had been stripped of the awards because of allegations that he had forfeited his amateur status by taking money to play baseball.

QUIZ: In 1979 the Lakers had two first-round draft choices. They selected Magic Johnson with one. Whom did they choose with the other?

Trivia Timeout

Jim Thorpe had a twin brother who died during childhood.

QUIZ ANSWER: Brad Holland of UCLA

JANUARY 19th

TODAY'S THOUGHT: "I don't think God gives a damn whether we hit or not. If God cared, Billy Graham would be hitting .400." —*Chris Sabo*

HISTORY: On this date in 1898 Brown shut out Harvard in the first intercollegiate hockey game.

QUIZ: Only one NHL team has won five consecutive Stanley Cups. Which one?

Trivia Timeout
In horse racing, the favorite finishes first less than 30 percent of the time.

QUIZ ANSWER: The Montreal Canadiens were the NHL champs from the 1955-56 season through 1959-60.

JANUARY 20th

TODAY'S THOUGHT: "As a nation we are dedicated to keeping physically fit — and parking as close to the stadium as possible." —*Bill Vaughan, writer*

HISTORY: On this date in 1968 the University of Houston ended UCLA's 47-game winning streak, defeating the Bruins, 71-69, in the first nationally televised college basketball game.

QUIZ: This NBA Hall of Famer was a three-time MVP in the ABA. Can you name him?

Trivia Timeout
Lew Alcindor declined to participate in the 1968 Olympics in support of the threatened black boycott of the Games.

QUIZ ANSWER: Julius Erving, who won the award in 1974, '75 and '76 (and in 1981 in the NBA)

JANUARY 21st

TODAY'S THOUGHT: "Through years of experience I have found that air offers less resistance than dirt." —*Jack Nicklaus, on why he tees up his ball so high*

HISTORY: On this date in 1975 the NHL All-Star game adopted an open door policy that marked the first time in pro sports history that reporters of both sexes had access to the player's locker room.

QUIZ: Do you recall the two boxing brothers who won Olympic gold medals as amateurs and the heavyweight championship as professionals?

Trivia Timeout

Before the NHL draft was implemented, the Montreal Canadiens had first dibs on any French-speaking player.

QUIZ ANSWER: Leon and Michael Spinks

JANUARY 22nd

TODAY'S THOUGHT: "The question isn't at what age I want to retire, it's at what income." —*George Foreman*

HISTORY: On this date in 1973 George Foreman pummeled Joe Frazier and captured the heavyweight crown with a second-round TKO in Kingston, Jamaica. Foreman reigned for 21 months before being dethroned by Muhammad Ali.

QUIZ: After George Foreman won the heavyweight gold medal in 1968, this Cuban boxer won the event in the next three Olympics. Can you name him?

Trivia Timeout

Jersey Joe Walcott is the only boxer to lose three consecutive heavyweight title fights.

QUIZ ANSWER: Teofilo Stevenson

JANUARY 23rd

TODAY'S THOUGHT: "I tell it like it is. Howard Cosell tells it like Roone Arledge wants it told." —*Harry Caray*

HISTORY: On this date in 1992 the "Mouth that Roared" was silenced. Howard Cosell announced his retirement from broadcasting.

QUIZ: In 1991 this third baseman became the first infielder to hit 30 or more home runs and steal 30 or more bases in the same season. Do you know his name?

Trivia Timeout

Lacrosse — a sport first played by North American Indians — is the national game of Canada.

QUIZ ANSWER: Howard Johnson hit 38 homers and stole 30 bases for the Mets that year.

JANUARY 24th

TODAY'S THOUGHT: "No game that can be played by a person with a wad of tobacco in his mouth is a sport." —*Andy Rooney*

HISTORY: On this date in 1955 the Major Leagues introduced baseball's equivalent of the shot clock, requiring that pitchers deliver the ball within 20 seconds.

QUIZ: What is the official distance in a marathon?

Trivia Timeout

Olympic gold medal gymnast Mary Lou Retton was the first female to appear on the front of a Wheaties box.

QUIZ ANSWER: A marathon is run over a course measuring 26 miles, 385 yards.

JANUARY 25th

TODAY'S THOUGHT: "I don't talk to kickers. What do you say to kickers? 'Kick'?" —*Joe Paterno*

HISTORY: On this date in 1924 the Winter Olympics debuted in Chamonix, France.

QUIZ: UCLA holds the record for the most consecutive wins in Division I men's basketball with 88. What team halted their streak in 1974?

Trivia Timeout

Speedskater Eric Heiden has been clocked at 31 miles per hour. Comparatively, the top recorded speed for a cheetah, the world's fastest animal, is 63 miles per hour.

QUIZ ANSWER: Notre Dame snapped the streak with a 71-70 victory over the Bruins. The last UCLA loss before that was in 1970 to...Notre Dame.

JANUARY 26th

TODAY'S THOUGHT: "Basketball...requires that the dictates of community prevail over selfish personal impulses." —*Bill Bradley*

HISTORY: On this date in 1960 Danny Heater of Burnsville, WV scored 135 points in a 32-minute high school basketball game. With Heater accounting for almost 80% of their offense and pulling down 32 rebounds, Burnsville "edged" Widen, 173-43.

QUIZ: What innovation of the American Basketball Association remained after the merger with the NBA?

Trivia Timeout

The Great Gretzky's pro hockey career began in 1978 with the Indianapolis Racers of the World Hockey Association.

QUIZ ANSWER: The three-point basket

JANUARY 27th

TODAY'S THOUGHT: "You can never overpay a good player. You can only overpay a bad one. I don't mind paying a good player $200,000. What I mind is paying a $20,000 ballplayer $22,000." —*Art Rooney*

HISTORY: On this date in 1944 Casey Stengel was fired as manager of the Boston Braves after five successive losing seasons.

QUIZ: Only two American league players have won the home run title six or more times. One was Babe Ruth. Do you know the other?

Trivia Timeout
The minimum depth of a golf hole is 4".

QUIZ ANSWER: Harmon Killebrew wore the crown six times between 1959 and 1967.

JANUARY 28th

TODAY'S THOUGHT: "Never tell 'em how many lettermen you've got coming back. Tell 'em how many you lost." —*Knute Rockne*

HISTORY: On this date in 1958 Roy Campanella's career was ended by a car crash that left him paralyzed. In his 10 years as the Brooklyn backstop, Campy was the National League MVP three times.

QUIZ: Who is the only two-time winner of the Heisman?

Trivia Timeout
The Heisman Trophy was named for Georgia Tech head coach John W. Heisman.

QUIZ ANSWER: Archie Griffin of Ohio State, who was named college football's best player in 1974 and '75

JANUARY 29th

TODAY'S THOUGHT: "I have only one superstition. I make sure I touch all the bases when I hit a home run." —*Babe Ruth*

HISTORY: On this date in 1936 the original members of the Baseball Hall of Fame were announced. The first inductees were Ty Cobb, Walter Johnson, Christy Mathewson, Babe Ruth and Honus Wagner.

QUIZ: The National Baseball Hall of Fame is located in Cooperstown, NY. Where are the football (professional) and basketball halls?

Trivia Timeout

Actor John Forsythe was once the public address announcer for the Brooklyn Dodgers at Ebbets Field.

QUIZ ANSWER: In Canton, OH and Springfield, MA

JANUARY 30th

TODAY'S THOUGHT: "The Super Bowl is our great national campfire around which we cluster." —*George Will*

HISTORY: On this date in 1983 Jack Kent Cooke's Washington Redskins defeated Miami in Super Bowl XVII. Since Cooke's Lakers had won the NBA crown in 1971-72, he became the only person to have owned championship-winning franchises in two major sports.

QUIZ: Who won the ABA's first scoring title?

Trivia Timeout

Tom Brown and Deion Sanders are the only men to have played in a Major League baseball game and in the Super Bowl.

QUIZ ANSWER: Connie Hawkins, in 1968

JANUARY 31st

TODAY'S THOUGHT: "It doesn't matter how many you walk just so long as they don't score." —*Nolan Ryan*

HISTORY: On this date in 1989 both teams left their defense in the locker room as Loyola Marymount defeated U.S. International, 181-150, in the highest-scoring college basketball game ever. Loyola's 181 points and their combined 331 points are records.

QUIZ: Whatever became of baseball's Seattle Pilots?

Trivia Timeout

On March 7, 1941 Los Animas (Colorado) High School edged La Junta, 2-0, in a boys basketball game. The first, final and deciding basket was scored in overtime!

QUIZ ANSWER: They sailed to Milwaukee and were rechristened the Brewers.

FEBRUARY 1st

TODAY'S THOUGHT: "If you can't beat 'em in the alley, you can't beat 'em on the ice." —*Conn Smythe, former Maple Leafs general manager*

HISTORY: On this date in 1970 New York Rangers goalie Terry Sawchuck blanked Pittsburgh, 6-0, for the 103rd and final shutout of his career. Sawchuck remains the only goalie in NHL history with over 100 shutouts.

QUIZ: Can you name the first NHL player to score 50 goals in a season?

Trivia Timeout

Baseball's 1991 Cy Young Award winner, Tom Glavine, was a 1984 fourth-round pick of the NHL's Los Angeles Kings.

QUIZ ANSWER: Maurice Richard of Montreal scored exactly 50 goals during the 1944-45 season.

FEBRUARY 2nd

TODAY'S THOUGHT: "I knew it was time to quit when I was chewing out an official and he walked off the penalty faster than I could keep up with him." —*George Halas*

HISTORY: On this date in 1876 organized professional baseball began with the formation of the National League.

QUIZ: Who was the Minnesota Vikings head coach when they entered the NFL in 1961?

Trivia Timeout

Hall of Famer Al Kaline is the only Major Leaguer to have over 300 career home runs, yet never hit 30 in a season.

QUIZ ANSWER: Norm Van Brocklin

FEBRUARY 3rd

TODAY'S THOUGHT: "Part of the charm of the Winter Olympics is that ice skating and all the rest of those Olympic sports completely disappear for four years at a time." —*Dan Jenkins, writer*

HISTORY: On this date in 1948 Dick Button became the first American skater to win the men's world figure skating title.

QUIZ: What American man won the World Figure Skating Championships from 1981 through 1984 and topped them off with the 1984 Olympic gold?

Trivia Timeout

"Sports Illustrated's" initial Sportsman of the Year, in 1954, was the world's first sub-four-minute miler, Roger Bannister.

QUIZ ANSWER: Scott Hamilton

FEBRUARY 4th

TODAY'S THOUGHT: "When you get hurt, everything hurts — hands, toes, fingers, everything. I can't even play golf. I sound like I'm making popcorn when I get up in the morning." —*Lawrence Taylor, on aging*

HISTORY: On this date in 1969 Bowie Kuhn was elected commissioner of Major League baseball. Kuhn was a compromise choice after a deadlock among supporters of Mike Burke and Chub Feeney.

QUIZ: This golfer won 11 consecutive tournaments in 1945. Can you name him?

Trivia Timeout

Former President Harry Truman had a bowling alley installed in the basement of the White House.

QUIZ ANSWER: Byron Nelson

FEBRUARY 5th

TODAY'S THOUGHT: "We weren't about stats. We were about winning." —*Magic Johnson, about himself and Larry Bird*

HISTORY: On this date in 1960 Boston Celtics center Bill Russell set an NBA record, pulling down 51 rebounds in a game against the Syracuse Nationals. The mark stood until the next season when Wilt Chamberlain wiped the glass — and the record off the books — with 55 boards against Russell and the Celtics.

QUIZ: True or false? Golf was once an Olympic event.

Trivia Timeout
The maximum weight of an official basketball is 22.9 ounces.

QUIZ ANSWER: True (in 1900 and 1904)

FEBRUARY 6th

TODAY'S THOUGHT: "Fear was absolutely necessary. Without it I would have been scared to death."
—*Floyd Patterson, former heavyweight champ*

HISTORY: On this date in 1925 basketball's longest winning streak came to an end. It wasn't the Lakers or UCLA. Passaic (NJ) High School won 159 straight games over five years before being tripped by Hackensack.

QUIZ: True or false? Babe Ruth once led the American League in earned run average (ERA) as a pitcher.

Trivia Timeout
Miami Heat coach Pat Riley was an 11th-round draft pick of the Dallas Cowboys in 1967.

QUIZ ANSWER: True. Ruth won the AL title with an ERA of 1.75 in 1916 while pitching for the Boston Red Sox.

FEBRUARY 7th

TODAY'S THOUGHT: "In my day, they just called you a bum." —*Joe DiMaggio, on fan vulgarity*

HISTORY: On this date in 1976 Darryl Sittler had the hot hand on the ice, setting an NHL record for points in a game. Sittler scored six goals and added four assists in Toronto's 11-4 win over Boston.

QUIZ: Who did Muhammad Ali defeat in his return to the ring after being stripped of his title?

Trivia Timeout
Author Rudyard Kipling invented the red golf ball for playing in snow.

QUIZ ANSWER: Ali began his quest to regain the heavyweight crown with a third-round knockout of Jerry Quarry.

FEBRUARY 8th

TODAY'S THOUGHT: "Everybody is an 'impact' player, whatever that means. History shows us that, for a lot of them, their only impact will be on the driver's seat of a truck." —*Jim Murray, writer, on the NFL draft*

HISTORY: On this date in 1936 the NFL conducted the first college draft.

QUIZ: Magic Johnson was the top pick in the 1979 NBA draft but didn't win Rookie of the Year. Who did?

Trivia Timeout
Hall of Famer Bill Russell was the second player chosen in the 1956 NBA draft. The Rochester Royals — armed with the first pick — gazed into their crystal ball and passed on Russell, choosing Si Green of Duquesne instead.

QUIZ ANSWER: Larry Bird of the Boston Celtics

FEBRUARY 9th

TODAY'S THOUGHT: "Throw peas at their knees and high riders in their eyes. Throw it in here when they're lookin' there and throw it there when they're lookin' in here." —*Satchel Paige*

HISTORY: On this date in 1971 Leroy "Satchel" Paige became the first member of the Negro League to be inducted into the Baseball Hall of Fame.

QUIZ: What slugger holds the Major League record for home runs by a switch-hitter?

Trivia Timeout

Joe DiMaggio's 56-game hitting streak included 56 singles and 56 runs scored.

QUIZ ANSWER: Mickey Mantle, with 536

FEBRUARY 10th

TODAY'S THOUGHT: "Boxing is a great sport and a dirty business." —*Ken Norton*

HISTORY: On this date in 1990 journeyman heavyweight Buster Douglas knocked Mike Tyson and the boxing world for a loop with a 10th-round knockout of the formerly-undefeated champ. The unheralded Douglas entered the fight as a 42-1 underdog.

QUIZ: Who was the youngest boxer to win the heavyweight title?

Trivia Timeout

Badminton began in India where it was originally called "poona".

QUIZ ANSWER: Mike Tyson, who was 20 when he won the crown in 1986

FEBRUARY 11th

TODAY'S THOUGHT: "It isn't enough for an umpire to merely know what he's doing. He has to look as though he knows what he's doing too."
—Larry Goetz, former NL umpire

HISTORY: On this date in 1968 Peggy Fleming won the women's figure skating gold medal at Grenoble, France.

QUIZ: Bob Mathias won the decathlon in two consecutive Olympics, earning the gold in 1948 and 1952. Who else accomplished this feat?

Trivia Timeout
Great Britain is the only country to participate in every Summer and Winter Olympics in the modern era.

QUIZ ANSWER: Daley Thompson of Great Britain, who went home with the gold in 1980 and '84

FEBRUARY 12th

TODAY'S THOUGHT: "Golf is not a sport. Golf is men in ugly pants walking." *—Rosie O'Donnell*

HISTORY: On this date in 1947 C.W. Stewart came up with a whopper of a fish tale — that's actually true. Fishing off the coast of Ecuador, Stewart caught a 221-pound Pacific sailfish, a record that still stands.

QUIZ: Three Major Leaguers have homered in eight consecutive games. Dale Long and Ken Griffey, Jr. are two. Who is the third?

Trivia Timeout
In the first Rose Bowl, Michigan defeated Stanford, 49-0, using only 11 players during the entire game.

QUIZ ANSWER: Don Mattingly

FEBRUARY 13th

TODAY'S THOUGHT: "It's hard to be a leader if nobody's following you." —*George Foster*

HISTORY: On this date in 1992 Don MacClean's 22 points led UCLA to victory over Oregon State and propelled him to the top as the all-time Bruin scoring leader. The record had stood at 2,325 points, a mark set by Kareem Abdul-Jabbar 22 years earlier.

QUIZ: Kareem Abdul-Jabbar is the NBA's all-time leading scorer. Who is in second place?

Trivia Timeout

The California (nee Los Angeles) Angels' first home was Wrigley Field — an old PCL park in LA.

QUIZ ANSWER: Wilt Chamberlain, with 31,419 career points versus Kareem Abdul-Jabbar's 38,387

FEBRUARY 14th

TODAY'S THOUGHT: "Never get married in the morning, 'cause you never know who you'll meet that night." —*Paul Hornung*

HISTORY: On this date in 1951 Sugar Ray Robinson knocked out Jake LaMotta to gain the middleweight title.

QUIZ: With what team did former Bills quarterback Jim Kelly make his professional debut?

Trivia Timeout

Sugar Ray Robinson's real name was Walker Smith. He adopted 'Ray Robinson' in the late 30's, borrowing it from another fighter. His nickname came from a sportswriter who described him as "the sweetest fighter...sweet as sugar".

QUIZ ANSWER: The Houston Gamblers of the USFL

FEBRUARY 15th

TODAY'S THOUGHT: "A successful coach is one who is still coaching." —*Ben Schwartzwalder*

HISTORY: On this date in 1991 Detroit Pistons coach Chuck Daly was picked to lead the 1992 U.S. Olympic basketball team. This marked the first time that NBA players were allowed to compete and the results were predictable. The "Dream Team" swept to the gold in Barcelona.

QUIZ: Do you recall the only New York Knick to win the NBA scoring title?

Trivia Timeout
The NBA's foul lane is 16' wide.

QUIZ ANSWER: Bernard King averaged 32.9 points per game to win the 1984-85 scoring title.

FEBRUARY 16th

TODAY'S THOUGHT: "They ought to play the women's finals on opening day. Everybody knows who's going to be in it." —*Jimmy Connors*

HISTORY: On this date in 1992 Martina Navratilova became tennis' all-time singles titles leader. Navratilova won her 158th career singles championship, beating Jana Novotna in the finals of the Virginia Slims.

QUIZ: In 1985 this 17-year old became the first unseeded player to win a men's singles final at Wimbledon. Who was it?

Trivia Timeout
A race horse's name can be no longer than eighteen letters.

QUIZ ANSWER: Boris Becker, who also was the first German man to win the event

FEBRUARY 17th

TODAY'S THOUGHT: "Pressure? Pressure is something that goes in tires." —*Charles Barkley*

HISTORY: On this date in 1992 the East Carolina women's basketball team made a beeline for the foul line in their game against American. The team took 58 free throws — an NCAA record — and sank 48 en route to a 100-81 win.

QUIZ: Jim Brown won the rushing title every year — but one — between 1957 and 1965. Who was the Green Bay Packer who led the NFL in rushing in 1962?

Trivia Timeout

The Campbell's Soup red and white label was inspired by the colors of the Cornell University football team.

QUIZ ANSWER: Jim Taylor

FEBRUARY 18th

TODAY'S THOUGHT: "It is necessary to relax your muscles when you can. Relaxing your brain is fatal." —*Sterling Moss, race driver*

HISTORY: On this date in 1979 Richard Petty drove his Oldsmobile an average of 143.977 mph to become the first man to win the Daytona 500 six times. Petty went on to take a seventh victory lap at Daytona before his retirement in 1992.

QUIZ: True or false? Tug of war was once an Olympic sport.

Trivia Timeout

The original Stanley cup was worth $48.67 when Lord Stanley of Preston donated it in 1893.

QUIZ ANSWER: True. It was discontinued in 1920.

FEBRUARY 19th

TODAY'S THOUGHT: "Once a guy starts wearing silk pajamas, it's hard to get up early." —*Eddie Arcaro, on the athlete's work ethic after the big money rolls in*

HISTORY: On this date in 1984 twins Phil and Steve Mahre finished first and second in the slalom at the Winter Olympics in Sarajevo, Yugoslavia. Phil turned in the better overall time to capture the gold.

QUIZ: Name the first female jockey to capture one of the jewels in racing's Triple Crown. Advance to the winner's circle if you can name the race and the horse.

Trivia Timeout
The only major sport that is a U.S. "original" is basketball.

QUIZ ANSWER: Julie Krone won the 1993 Belmont Stakes aboard Colonial Affair.

FEBRUARY 20th

TODAY'S THOUGHT: "Players sometimes benefit from a change of scenery. Well, good players can benefit from a change of scenery. Bad players are bad players wherever they are." —*Doug Moe*

HISTORY: On this date in 1988 Boitano bested Orser in the "Battle of the Brians" at the Winter Olympics in Calgary. American Brian Boitano's performance in the free skate program proved to be the margin of victory over Canadian Brian Orser for the gold medal.

QUIZ: Who holds the American League record for the most RBI's in a season?

Trivia Timeout
Bowling pins are 12" apart.

QUIZ ANSWER: Lou Gehrig, with 184 in 1931

FEBRUARY 21st

TODAY'S THOUGHT: "The race is not always to the swift, nor the battle to the strong, but that's the way to bet." —*Damon Runyon*

HISTORY: On this date in 1993 Indiana's Greg Graham scored 32 points against Purdue but made only two field goals. Graham set a Big Ten record by making 26 free throws in the Hoosier's 93-78 victory.

QUIZ: I made 21 of 22 shots in leading UCLA to victory over Memphis State in the 1973 NCAA basketball tournament final.

Trivia Timeout

In tennis the term "love", meaning zero, comes from the French "l'oeuf" which means egg, as in goose egg.

QUIZ ANSWER: Bill Walton

FEBRUARY 22nd

TODAY'S THOUGHT: "It is the child of avarice, the brother of iniquity, and the father of mischief." —*George Washington, on gambling*

HISTORY: On this date in 1980 a "miracle on ice" took place in Lake Placid, NY. The U.S. Olympic hockey team upset the heavily-favored Soviets, 4-3, to advance to the finals against Finland.

QUIZ: Who is the only man in All-Star history to suffer losses as both the American and National League manager?

Trivia Timeout

Former Minnesota Vikings' placekicker Fred Cox invented the Nerf Ball.

QUIZ ANSWER: Sparky Anderson

FEBRUARY 23rd

TODAY'S THOUGHT: "The Dodgers move out of Brooklyn? Impossible."
— *"Sports Illustrated", March 4, 1957 issue*

HISTORY: On this date in 1960 a wrecking ball painted to resemble a baseball reduced Ebbets Field to rubble, three years after O'Malley's Dodgers packed up and headed west.

QUIZ: Who was the first Los Angeles hurler to pitch a no-hitter at Dodger Stadium?

Trivia Timeout

Yankee manager Bill Virdon never managed a game in Yankee Stadium. During Virdon's tenure, the "Bronx Bombers" played at Shea Stadium in Queens.

QUIZ ANSWER: Bo Belinsky of the Los Angeles Angels, who did it in 1962

FEBRUARY 24th

TODAY'S THOUGHT: "Everyone has some fear. A man who has no fear belongs in a mental hospital. Or on special teams." —*Walt Michaels, former Jets' head coach*

HISTORY: On this date in 1985 quarterback Jim Kelly of the USFL's Houston Gamblers set a pro football record, passing for 574 yards in a win over the Los Angeles Express.

QUIZ: When John Wooden won his first NCAA title in 1964, what team did UCLA defeat in the final?

Trivia Timeout

From 1949 to 1951 the Temple Owl's basketball program featured a player known as "the Owl without a vowel" — William M-l-k-v-y.

QUIZ ANSWER: Duke

FEBRUARY 25th

TODAY'S THOUGHT: "I zigged when I should have zagged." —*Jack Roper, after being KO'd by Joe Louis*

HISTORY: On this date in 1964 Muhammad Ali — then fighting as Cassius Clay — stunned the boxing world when he captured the heavyweight title. Clay was declared the winner when Sonny Liston failed to answer the bell for the seventh round in their first meeting, in Miami.

QUIZ: What boxer did Sonny Liston beat to become the world heavyweight champion?

Trivia Timeout
After Wyatt Earp retired as marshal of Tombstone, Arizona he moved to San Francisco and became a boxing referee.

QUIZ ANSWER: Liston KO'd Floyd Patterson in 1962.

FEBRUARY 26th

TODAY'S THOUGHT: "I always felt the more Browns that I could place on other teams, the better off I'd be." —*Bill Veeck, then owner of the inept St. Louis Browns*

HISTORY: On this date in 1991 the veterans committee elected Bill Veeck and Tony Lazzeri to the Baseball Hall of Fame.

QUIZ: In 1955 I became the youngest American League player to win a batting title. Who am I?

Trivia Timeout
Only two "charter" NBA teams have remained in their original cities, the New York Knicks and the Boston Celtics.

QUIZ ANSWER: Al Kaline, at age 20, batted .340 for the Detroit Tigers and also contributed 27 home runs, 102 RBI's and 121 runs.

FEBRUARY 27th

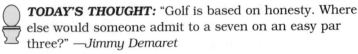

TODAY'S THOUGHT: "Golf is based on honesty. Where else would someone admit to a seven on an easy par three?" —*Jimmy Demaret*

HISTORY: On this date in 1992 Tiger Woods became the youngest golfer ever to play in a PGA Tour event. Woods was just two months past his 16th birthday when he teed off at the Los Angeles Open.

QUIZ: Which golfer is the only six-time winner of the Masters?

Trivia Timeout

Gene Sarazen, Walter Hagen and Gary Player competed in 22 consecutive U.S. Opens without missing a cut.

QUIZ ANSWER: Jack Nicklaus, who won the tournament in 1963, '65, '66, '72, '75 and '86

FEBRUARY 28th

TODAY'S THOUGHT: "Nobody roots for Goliath." —*Wilt Chamberlain*

HISTORY: On this date in 1967 Wilt Chamberlain finally missed a shot — after 11 days and 35 straight field goals, a new NBA record. Another NBA record was set 14 years later when Calvin Murphy missed a free throw after 78 successful attempts.

QUIZ: Besides Dean Smith, who is the only man to play on and later coach a basketball team to the NCAA title?

Trivia Timeout

Wilt Chamberlain never fouled out of a game in his 14-year pro career.

QUIZ ANSWER: Bobby Knight, who played with Ohio State and coached Indiana

FEBRUARY 29th

TODAY'S THOUGHT: "I know, but I had a better year than Hoover." —*Babe Ruth, after his $80,000 salary was compared to the president's $75,000*

HISTORY: On this date in 1972 Henry Aaron signed a new contract with the Braves, making him the first Major League player to earn $200,000 a year.

QUIZ: Who was the last American woman to win the Olympic gold medal in figure skating?

Trivia Timeout

Only right-handed players can play polo according to the U.S. Polo Association. The governing body made the ruling in 1974 to cut down on collisions between lefties and righties.

QUIZ ANSWER: Tara Lipinski, in 1998

MARCH 1st

TODAY'S THOUGHT: "I figure anybody hits you, you should hit him back. Isn't that the way the game's supposed to be played?" —*Bobby Clarke, on hockey*

HISTORY: On this date in 1988 Wayne Gretzky set a new NHL career record for assists in the Edmonton Oilers' 5-3 win over Los Angeles. Gretzky tallied his 1,050th assist in less than nine seasons, breaking a mark that took Gordie Howe 26 years to establish.

QUIZ: What coach led the 1980 U.S. Olympic hockey team to the gold at Lake Placid?

Trivia Timeout

Former NFL commissioner Pete Rozelle's real first name was Alvin.

QUIZ ANSWER: Herb Brooks

MARCH 2nd

TODAY'S THOUGHT: "To win you have to risk loss." —*Jean-Claude Killy*

HISTORY: On this date in 1962 Wilt Chamberlain made 36 field goals and 28 free throws to become the only pro player to score 100 points in a game as the Philadelphia Warriors outgunned the New York Knicks, 169-147.

QUIZ: Milwaukee won a coin toss in the 1969 NBA draft for the right to select Kareem Abdul-Jabbar with the first pick. Which team lost the toss?

Trivia Timeout

Tycoon J. Paul Getty was once a sparring partner for Jack Dempsey.

QUIZ ANSWER: The Phoenix Suns, who settled for Neal Walk

MARCH 3rd

TODAY'S THOUGHT: "No one has ever bet enough on a winning horse." —*Richard Sasuly*

HISTORY: On this date in 1985 Bill Shoemaker rode Lord at War to victory in the Santa Anita Handicap and became the first jockey to win $100 million in purses.

QUIZ: The NHL grew from six teams to 12 in 1967. Which of the expansion clubs was the first to win a Stanley Cup?

Trivia Timeout

A thoroughbred racehorse is tattooed with an identification number under its upper lip.

QUIZ ANSWER: The Philadelphia Flyers won the Cup in 1974 and again in 1975.

MARCH 4th

TODAY'S THOUGHT: "One man practicing sportsmanship is far better than 50 preaching it." —*Knute Rockne*

HISTORY: On this date in 1941 Chicago goalie Sam LoPresti stopped a record 80 of 83 shots on goal in a game against Montreal. But the three shots that got by him were enough to give the Canadiens a 3-2 win.

QUIZ: In what year was golf's British Open first held?

Trivia Timeout

"Gymnasium" stems from the Greek word "gymnos" which means "naked". And that's how the ancient Greek athletes practiced — in the raw.

QUIZ ANSWER: 1860 — Eight players entered, playing three twelve-hole rounds each

MARCH 5th

TODAY'S THOUGHT: "It's impossible to imagine Goethe or Beethoven being good at billiards or golf." —*H.L. Mencken*

HISTORY: On this date in 1984 Brigham Young quarterback Steve Young signed a $42 million contract with the Los Angeles Express of the USFL. Unfortunately, the league folded later that year. Fortunately, for Young, his contract was guaranteed.

QUIZ: What game is divided into periods which are called "chukkers"?

Trivia Timeout

A hockey puck, made of vulcanized rubber, weighs six ounces.

QUIZ ANSWER: Polo

MARCH 6th

TODAY'S THOUGHT: "Statistics are used by baseball fans in much the same way that a drunk leans against a street lamp; it's there more for support than enlightenment." —*Vin Scully*

HISTORY: On this date in 1976 Dorothy Hamill became the first American woman in eight years to win the world figure skating championship.

QUIZ: In my NBA career I was Rookie of the Year, MVP and later head coach for the same franchise. Who am I?

Trivia Timeout

Only 18 balls were hit out of Pittsburgh's Forbes Field in the park's 61-year history. Willie Stargell hit seven of them.

QUIZ ANSWER: Wes Unseld pulled off this basketball "hat trick" for the Bullets.

MARCH 7th

TODAY'S THOUGHT: "You drive the car, you don't carry it." —*Janet Guthrie, Indy driver, on her physical ability to compete*

HISTORY: On this date in 1970 Notre Dame guard Austin Carr scored 61 points in a 112-82 win over Ohio University. Carr's effort broke the NCAA tournament single-game scoring record set five years earlier by Bill Bradley of Princeton.

QUIZ: What's the first name of golfer Tiger Woods?

Trivia Timeout
Of the top ten NCAA Tournament single-game scoring performances, Austin Carr is responsible for five of them. In that 1970 tourney, he averaged 52.7 points per game.

QUIZ ANSWER: Eldrick

MARCH 8th

TODAY'S THOUGHT: "No one knows what to say in the loser's locker room." —*Muhammad Ali*

HISTORY: On this date in 1970 unbeaten heavyweight champ Joe Frazier retained his title with a 15-round unanimous decision over Muhammad Ali at Madison Square Garden. Frazier and Ali met twice more, with Ali winning both fights.

QUIZ: What three fighters defeated Sugar Ray Leonard during his professional boxing career?

Trivia Timeout
Table tennis balls have been known to travel off the paddle at speeds exceeding 100 mph.

QUIZ ANSWER: Roberto Duran, Terry Norris and Hector "Macho" Camacho

MARCH 9th

TODAY'S THOUGHT: "Jogging is very beneficial. It's good for your legs and your feet. It's also good for the ground. It makes it feel needed." —*Snoopy*

HISTORY: On this date in 1981 the Buffalo Sabres entered the NHL record book when they scored nine goals in one period.

QUIZ: In 1922 he became the only player in Major League history to hit 40 home runs and bat .400 in the same season. What's his name?

Trivia Timeout

The odds of making a hole-in-one in golf are 10,738:1.

QUIZ ANSWER: Rogers Hornsby, with 42 homers and a .401 average

MARCH 10th

TODAY'S THOUGHT: "Playing baseball for a living is like having a license to steal." —*Pete Rose*

HISTORY: On this date in 1963 rookie second baseman Pete Rose made his debut for the Cincinnati Reds, doubling twice in an exhibition game against the Chicago White Sox.

QUIZ: Jackie Robinson was Major League baseball's first black player. Who was second?

Trivia Timeout

Long before he got into big trouble for tax evasion, Pete Rose got into a little trouble for parking illegally outside Cincinnati's Riverfront Stadium. The street name on the ticket...Pete Rose Way.

QUIZ ANSWER: Larry Doby

MARCH 11th

TODAY'S THOUGHT: "The problem is when you get it, you're too damned old to do anything about it."
—Jimmy Connors, on experience

HISTORY: On this date in 1990 Jennifer Capriati became the youngest player to reach the finals of a major pro tennis tournament. The 13-year-old lost to Gabriela Sabatini, 6-4, 7-5, at the Virginia Slims of Florida, her first event after turning pro.

QUIZ: Who holds the NBA record for most All-Star game appearances?

Trivia Timeout
The name of the skier shown crashing in the introduction to ABC's "Wide World of Sports" is Vinko Bogataj.

QUIZ ANSWER: Kareem Abdul-Jabbar, with 18

MARCH 12th

TODAY'S THOUGHT: "I consider playing basketball...the most shallow thing in the world."
—Bill Russell

HISTORY: On this date in 1956 NBA guard Dick Farley had his 15 minutes of fame. Make that five minutes. That's how long it took Farley to foul out of a game between his Syracuse Nationals and the St. Louis Hawks.

QUIZ: What is the most popular nickname for college football teams?

Trivia Timeout
Jim Thorpe won the pentathlon in the 1912 Olympics. The fifth place finisher was George S. Patton, the future U.S. general.

QUIZ ANSWER: Tigers — 28 major teams use it.

MARCH 13th

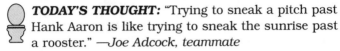

TODAY'S THOUGHT: "Trying to sneak a pitch past Hank Aaron is like trying to sneak the sunrise past a rooster." —*Joe Adcock, teammate*

HISTORY: On this date in 1954 Braves starting outfielder Bobby Thomson fractured his ankle during an exhibition game, opening a spot in the lineup for a 20-year-old rookie named Henry Aaron.

QUIZ: Who is the only Brave to have played for the team in Boston, Milwaukee and Atlanta?

Trivia Timeout

Hank Aaron won the NL home run crown four times. Three of the four times, he finished the year with 44 homers — the number on his uniform.

QUIZ ANSWER: Hall of Famer Eddie Mathews

MARCH 14th

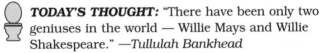

TODAY'S THOUGHT: "There have been only two geniuses in the world — Willie Mays and Willie Shakespeare." —*Tullulah Bankhead*

HISTORY: On this date in 1967 the AFL and NFL held their first combined draft.

QUIZ: Joe Namath and Gale Sayers were the 11th and 12th-place finishers in the 1964 Heisman Trophy balloting. A Notre Dame QB won the award. Who was it?

Trivia Timeout

Et tu, Pittsburgh? The Steelers made Notre Dame quarterback William Shakespeare their first pick in the 1936 NFL draft.

QUIZ ANSWER: John Huarte, who, like Namath, was signed by the New York Jets

MARCH 15th

TODAY'S THOUGHT: "Exercise is bunk. If you are healthy, you don't need it; if you are sick, you shouldn't take it." —*Henry Ford*

HISTORY: On this date in 1970 Bobby Orr of the Boston Bruins became the first NHL defenseman to score 100 points in a season.

QUIZ: Of the ten goalies with the most career NHL wins, only one has a losing record. Can you identify him?

Trivia Timeout
The bases in baseball measure 15" x 15" —excluding home, of course.

QUIZ ANSWER: Gump Worsley, who finished his career with 335 wins, 353 losses and 150 ties

MARCH 16th

TODAY'S THOUGHT: "Playgrounds are the best place to learn the game because if you lose, you sit down." —*Gary Williams, college basketball coach*

HISTORY: On this date in 1938 Temple beat Colorado, 60-36, to win the first National Invitation Tournament and the collegiate basketball championship. The NCAA staged its own tourney the following year.

QUIZ: Name the only school to win the NIT and the NCAA in the same year.

Trivia Timeout
The first NCAA champion was Oregon. They defeated Ohio State 46-33.

QUIZ ANSWER: City College of New York won both tournaments at the end of the 1949-50 season.

MARCH 17th

TODAY'S THOUGHT: "Baseball is what we were. Football is what we've become."
—*Mary McGrory, columnist*

HISTORY: On this date in 1886 "The Sporting News" published its first issue. Copies sold for five cents each.

QUIZ: Before embarking on a pro basketball career, Danny Ainge tried his hand at baseball. Do you remember with what Major League team he played?

Trivia Timeout

A recent study concluded that the magazine most likely to be stolen from public libraries in the U.S. is "Sports Illustrated".

QUIZ ANSWER: The Toronto Blue Jays

MARCH 18th

TODAY'S THOUGHT: "My only feeling about superstition is that it's unlucky to be behind at the end of the game." —*Duffy Daugherty*

HISTORY: On this date in 1945 Maurice "The Rocket" Richard scored his 50th goal of the season, a first in the NHL.

QUIZ: What was former U.S. Senator Bill Bradley's nickname in the NBA?

Trivia Timeout

Forrest Smithson, an American theology student, lodged a protest against Sunday competition in the 1908 Olympic Games by carrying a Bible during the 100 meter hurdles. Smithson won the race.

QUIZ ANSWER: "Dollar" Bill

MARCH 19th

TODAY'S THOUGHT: "I've got a theory that if you give 100 percent all the time, somehow things work out in the end." —*Larry Bird*

HISTORY: On this date in 1960 Ohio State defeated defending champion California, 75-55, to win the NCAA tournament. The Buckeyes were led by future NBA Hall of Famers Jerry Lucas and John Havlicek.

QUIZ: Apart from Wilt Chamberlain and Bill Russell, only two NBA players have grabbed 40 or more rebounds in a game. Can you name either man?

Trivia Timeout
On the bench for that OSU team was a reserve guard named Bobby Knight.

QUIZ ANSWER: Jerry Lucas and Nate Thurmond

MARCH 20th

TODAY'S THOUGHT: "There's no such thing as coulda, shoulda and woulda. If you shoulda and coulda, you woulda done it." —*Pat Riley*

HISTORY: On this date in 1973 Roberto Clemente was elected to the Baseball Hall of Fame. Clemente's induction came less than three months after his death in a plane crash while delivering relief supplies to earthquake victims in Nicaragua.

QUIZ: What was the original name of the Houston Astros?

Trivia Timeout
The score of a forfeited softball game is 7-0.

QUIZ ANSWER: Houston entered the National League as the Colt .45's.

MARCH 21st

TODAY'S THOUGHT: "The secret of managing is to keep the guys who hate you away from the guys who are undecided." —*Casey Stengel*

HISTORY: On this date in 1953 Boston outlasted Syracuse, 111-105, in an NBA playoff game that stretched into four overtime periods. A total of 12 players fouled out of the contest, including seven Celtics.

QUIZ: Only three Pittsburgh Pirates have ever won home run titles. Terry Leach did it in 1902. Can you recall those other two Buc sluggers?

Trivia Timeout
Walter Johnson holds the career record for hit batsmen—206.

QUIZ ANSWER: Ralph Kiner and Willie Stargell

MARCH 22nd

TODAY'S THOUGHT: "Never let fear of striking out get in your way." —*Babe Ruth*

HISTORY: On this date in 1969 Lew Alcindor was named MVP of the NCAA championship game for the third year in a row. The UCLA center led his Bruin teammates to a 92-72 win over Purdue by dumping in 37 points.

QUIZ: The AFL began play in 1960. That same year, the NFL expanded by one team. What team was added?

Trivia Timeout
The official state sport of Maryland is jousting.

QUIZ ANSWER: The Dallas Cowboys

MARCH 23rd

TODAY'S THOUGHT: "You've got to be in position for luck to happen. Luck doesn't go around looking for a stumblebum." —*Darrell Royal*

HISTORY: On this date in 1952 Chicago's Bill Mosienko scored three goals faster than you could say "hat trick". Mosienko's goals all came within 21 seconds in the third period in a 7-6 win over the Rangers.

QUIZ: Who was the first pitcher to throw a complete game, 1-0 victory in the seventh game of a World Series?

Trivia Timeout

Kansas City Chiefs owner Lamar Hunt coined the term "Super Bowl".

QUIZ ANSWER: Ralph Terry, who blanked the San Francisco Giants in the '62 Series

MARCH 24th

TODAY'S THOUGHT: "Publicity is like poison—it won't hurt you if you don't swallow it."
—*Joe Paterno*

HISTORY: On this date in 1962 Emile Griffith regained the welterweight title with a 12th-round knockout of Benny "Kid" Paret. Tragedy struck when Paret died less than two weeks later from injuries sustained in the fight.

QUIZ: Of all the players who spent their entire careers with one team, who has the most home runs?

Trivia Timeout

Women weren't allowed to attend boxing matches until 1916.

QUIZ ANSWER: Mike Schmidt, who hit 548 homers during his career with the Phillies

MARCH 25th

TODAY'S THOUGHT: "I have gotten weary of sports. You have to if you've got a mind and if you're an educated man." —*Howard Cosell*

HISTORY: On this date in 1973 a season of futility finally ended for the Philadelphia 76ers. A loss gave the team a 9-73 record, the worst in NBA history.

QUIZ: Can you name the mascots of the Army, Navy and Air Force football teams?

Trivia Timeout

A couple of guys with the "right stuff" participated together in U.S. bombing missions over Korea. Co-piloting with Hall of Famer Ted Williams was astronaut John Glenn.

QUIZ ANSWER: The Army has its mule, the Navy its goat and the Air Force mascot is a falcon.

MARCH 26th

TODAY'S THOUGHT: "It makes as much sense as a secretary going home and spending her nights typing." —*Walter Payton, on why he doesn't watch "Monday Night Football"*

HISTORY: On this date in 1979 Michigan State defeated Indiana State, 75-64, to win the NCAA Tournament.

QUIZ: Four USC tailbacks have won the Heisman. Marcus Allen won it in 1981. Name the other three.

Trivia Timeout

Timekeepers estimate that the action in a 60-minute football game actually amounts to 14 minutes.

QUIZ ANSWER: Mike Garrett (1965), O.J. Simpson (1968) and Charles White (1979)

MARCH 27th

TODAY'S THOUGHT: "It's not so much a sporting event as a deathwatch. They hold it, fittingly, on Memorial Day." —*Jim Murray, on the Indianapolis 500*

HISTORY: On this date in 1917 the Stanley Cup was first awarded to the best team in professional hockey as the Seattle Metropolitans bested the Montreal Canadiens. Until that time, the cup had been given to amateur teams.

QUIZ: Name the two four-time winners of the Indy 500.

Trivia Timeout
Sean Connery, a.k.a. James Bond, was given locker number 007 when he joined Los Angeles' exclusive Lake Sherwood Country Club.

QUIZ ANSWER: A.J. Foyt and Al Unser

MARCH 28th

TODAY'S THOUGHT: "This (defeat) has taught me a lesson, but I'm not sure what it is." —*John McEnroe*

HISTORY: On this date in 1993 the United States became the first Davis Cup defender to lose in the first round. Australia beat the U.S. tennis squad, 4-1.

QUIZ: This pair of brothers are the only siblings to have thrown nine-inning no-hitters in the Major Leagues. Who are they?

Trivia Timeout
The NBA regular season is 82 games, but in 1991-92, Thurl Bailey played in 84. He played in 13 games for the Utah Jazz and then was traded to the Minnesota Timberwolves where he participated in 71 more.

QUIZ ANSWER: Ken and Bob Forsch

MARCH 29th

TODAY'S THOUGHT: "When you can do it out there between the white lines, you can live any way you want." —*Denny McLain*

HISTORY: On this date in 1982 coach Dean Smith of North Carolina won his first NCAA tournament.

QUIZ: In 1976, '77 and '80 three different former UCLA centers led the NBA in rebounding. Can you get this trio?

Trivia Timeout

A.C. Gilbert was a United States pole vaulter in the 1908 Olympics. A year later he was scaling new heights with his invention of the Erector Set.

QUIZ ANSWER: Kareem Abdul-Jabbar ('76), Bill Walton ('77) and Swen Nater ('80)

MARCH 30th

TODAY'S THOUGHT: "The bowling alley is the poor man's country club." —*Sanford Hansell*

HISTORY: On this date in 1992 Pat Swilling became the highest-paid defensive player in NFL history. The New Orleans Saints matched a three-year, $5 million+ contract offer by the Detroit Lions to keep the linebacker.

QUIZ: Who is the only man to have won the World Series MVP award with two different teams?

Trivia Timeout

The official name for the bird in badminton is the "shuttlecock".

QUIZ ANSWER: "Mr. October", Reggie Jackson, won it with the A's in 1973 and the Yankees in 1977.

MARCH 31st

TODAY'S THOUGHT: "Build up your weaknesses and they become your strong points." —*Knute Rockne*

HISTORY: On this date in 1931 a plane crash in Kansas claimed the life of Notre Dame football coach Knute Rockne at the age of 42. The Fighting Irish won six national championships during Rockne's 13-year tenure.

QUIZ: In what states did the following ABA teams play?
A: Colonels   B: Squires   C: Chaparrals

Trivia Timeout

Candlestick Park, home to the San Francisco Giants, was the site of the last performance of the Beatles, on August 19, 1966.

QUIZ ANSWER: A—Kentucky; B—Virginia; C—The Dallas Chaparrals played in Texas.

APRIL 1st

TODAY'S THOUGHT: "There are two theories on hitting the knuckleball. Unfortunately, neither of them works." —*Charlie Lau*

HISTORY: On this date in 1972 the baseball players staged the first strike in the sport's history. The walkout, no April Fool's joke, lasted 13 days.

QUIZ: In what movie did Gene Hackman play the coach of a small-town high school basketball team that made the big time by winning the state championship?

Trivia Timeout

Harry "Slug" Heilman was an odd hitter. The Detroit Tigers slugger won the American League batting title every other year from 1921-27.

QUIZ ANSWER: "Hoosiers"

APRIL 2nd

TODAY'S THOUGHT: "Fly fishing may be a very pleasant amusement; but angling or boat fishing I can only compare to a stick and a string, with a worm at one end and a fool at the other." —*Dr. Samuel Johnson*

HISTORY: On this date in 1983 Chicago defensive back Luther Bradley intercepted six passes in a USFL game against Tampa Bay.

QUIZ: Where did the NBA's Utah Jazz play their home games before they moved to Salt Lake City?

Trivia Timeout

Yankee Stadium opened in 1923. Before that time, the "Bronx Bombers" played in Manhattan's Polo Grounds.

QUIZ ANSWER: New Orleans (hence, the nickname "Jazz")

APRIL 3rd

TODAY'S THOUGHT: "Pro football is a mean game, ideally played by mean men. If it builds character, so does street mugging." —*Larry King*

HISTORY: On this date in 1989 Michigan beat Seton Hall, 80-79, in overtime to win the NCAA basketball championship, as the Wolverines' Rumeal Robinson sank two free throws with three seconds left. This nail-biter was the first title game to go into OT in 26 years.

QUIZ: In 1984 I threw 48 touchdown passes, breaking the NFL mark of 36 held by George Blanda. Who am I?

Trivia Timeout
Arnold Palmer won at least one PGA Tour event each year from 1955-1971.

QUIZ ANSWER: Dan Marino of the Miami Dolphins

APRIL 4th

TODAY'S THOUGHT: "I didn't say everything I said I did." —*Yogi Berra*

HISTORY: On this date in 1988 Toronto's George Bell became the first man in baseball history to hit three home runs on Opening Day. Bret Saberhagen and the Royals were the victims in the Blue Jays' 5-3 win.

QUIZ: Who was the last American to win an Olympic marathon?

Trivia Timeout
Ernest Lawrence Thayer received $5 for writing the poem "Casey at the Bat" in 1888.

QUIZ ANSWER: Frank Shorter won the gold medal in Munich in 1972.

APRIL 5th

TODAY'S THOUGHT: "The qualities and capacities that are important in running — such factors as will power, the ability to apply effort during extreme fatigue, and the acceptance of pain — have a radiating power that subtly influences one's life." —*James Fixx*

HISTORY: On this date in 1984 Kareem Abdul-Jabbar surpassed Wilt Chamberlain to become the NBA's all-time leading scorer.

QUIZ: Name the only horse to have won the Kentucky Derby in less than two minutes.

Trivia Timeout

Pigs can run a 7-1/2 minute mile.

QUIZ ANSWER: Secretariat finished in 1:59-2/5 in 1973.

APRIL 6th

TODAY'S THOUGHT: "We've all been blessed with God-given talents. Mine just happens to be beating people up." —*Sugar Ray Leonard*

HISTORY: On this date in 1987 Sugar Ray Leonard became the middleweight champion of the world with a 12-round decision over Marvelous Marvin Hagler.

QUIZ: George Brett of the Royals was the batter in the infamous "pine tar incident". Who was the pitcher?

Trivia Timeout

Four holes-in-one were made in the U.S. Open at Rochester, New York's Oak Hill Country Club on June 16, 1989.

QUIZ ANSWER: The Yankees' Goose Gossage yielded the home run that was nullified by the umpires, thus enraging Brett.

APRIL 7th

TODAY'S THOUGHT: "Success isn't permanent and failure isn't fatal." —*Mike Ditka*

HISTORY: On this date in 1979 Ken Forsch of the Houston Astros hurled an early-season no-hitter, blanking Atlanta, 6-0.

QUIZ: The best won-lost record for a season in the American League is 111-43. Which team compiled it and in what year?

Trivia Timeout

In a 1963 basketball game in Alabama, West End High School defeated Glen Vocational, 97-54. Walter Garrett scored every single point for the victors.

QUIZ ANSWER: The Cleveland Indians established this all-time mark in 1954.

APRIL 8th

TODAY'S THOUGHT: "The pitcher has got only a ball, I've got the bat. So the percentage in weapons is in my favor and I let the fellow with the ball do the fretting." —*Henry Aaron*

HISTORY: On this date in 1974 Hank Aaron hit a 1-0 pitch off Al Downing into the left field bull pen for career home run #715, breaking the record held by Babe Ruth.

QUIZ: What's the distance from the pitcher's rubber to home plate?

Trivia Timeout

In baseball, a ball that landed in fair territory and bounced into the stands was counted as a home run until 1931.

QUIZ ANSWER: 60 feet, 6 inches

APRIL 9th

TODAY'S THOUGHT: "Let's play two!" —*Ernie Banks*

HISTORY: On this date in 1959 the Boston Celtics defeated the Minneapolis Lakers, 118-113, to capture the NBA crown in four straight games. This was the first sweep in championship play and the first of a record eight consecutive NBA titles for the Celtics.

QUIZ: What year was the first World Series game played in California? Which teams were involved?

Trivia Timeout

The stripes on an NFL official's uniform are two inches wide.

QUIZ ANSWER: The Los Angeles Dodgers and the Chicago White Sox went west with the World Series in 1959.

APRIL 10th

TODAY'S THOUGHT: "There are three types of people...people who make things happen, people who watch things happen and people who don't know what's happening." —*John Madden*

HISTORY: On this date in 1962 the expansion Houston Colt .45's won the first regular-season Major League game played in Texas, downing the Cubs, 11-2.

QUIZ: True or false? Bo Jackson is the only NFL player with two rushing touchdowns of 90 yards or more.

Trivia Timeout

Rotisserie baseball was cooked up by inventor Daniel Okrent in 1980.

QUIZ ANSWER: True. Jackson rushed for a 91-yard TD in 1987 and he scored on a 90-yard run in 1989.

APRIL 11th

TODAY'S THOUGHT: "I've come to the conclusion that the two most important things in life are good friends and a good bullpen." —*Bob Lemon, Hall of Fame pitcher*

HISTORY: On this date in 1980 two California Angels teammates combined to no-hit the Seattle Mariners. Mark Langston pitched seven innings before Mike Witt hurled the final two frames in the 1-0 win.

QUIZ: Who is the only woman to have won nine singles titles at Wimbledon?

Trivia Timeout
Softball was originally called kitten ball.

QUIZ ANSWER: Martina Navratilova, who was champion in 1978 and '79, 1982-87 and 1990

APRIL 12th

TODAY'S THOUGHT: "Officiating is the only occupation in the world where the highest accolade is silence." —*Earl Strom, NBA referee*

HISTORY: On this date in 1958 Bob Pettit scored 50 points to lead the St. Louis Hawks to a 110-109 victory over the Boston Celtics for the NBA championship.

QUIZ: Wayne Gretzky set the NHL record for most goals in a season in 1981-82. How many goals did the "Great One" score?

Trivia Timeout
Before 1859 baseball umpires sat behind home plate in rocking chairs.

QUIZ ANSWER: Gretzky tallied 92 goals.

APRIL 13th

TODAY'S THOUGHT: "I don't trust doctors. They are like golfers. Every one has a different answer to your problems." —*Seve Ballesteros*

HISTORY: On this date in 1986 46-year old Jack Nicklaus became the oldest player to win The Masters tournament.

QUIZ: Can you name the only school to win the NCAA men's basketball championship that is not located in any of the 50 states?

Trivia Timeout

Jack Dempsey entered the ring at age 18, boxing under the name "Kid Blackie".

QUIZ ANSWER: Georgetown University, which is located in the District of Columbia

APRIL 14th

TODAY'S THOUGHT: "The rhythms of the game are so similar to the pattern of American life. Periods of leisure, interrupted by bursts of frantic activity."
—*Roger Kahn, on baseball*

HISTORY: On this date in 1960 Montreal set an NHL record that is yet to be matched. Sweeping Toronto, 4-0, the Canadiens captured their fifth Stanley Cup in a row.

QUIZ: Who was the last Major League pitcher to win 30 or more games in a season? How many did he win?

Trivia Timeout

Muhammad Ali wore a "lucky" robe to his fights, one of which was given to him by Elvis Presley.

QUIZ ANSWER: Denny McLain of the Detroit Tigers went 31-6 in 1968.

APRIL 15th

TODAY'S THOUGHT: "I figured that someday I'd have to meet my Maker and that He'd ask me why I didn't let that boy play. I was afraid that if I told Him it was because he was black, that wouldn't be sufficient." —*Happy Chandler, former baseball commissioner, on Jackie Robinson*

HISTORY: On this date in 1947 Jackie Robinson broke the color barrier in Major League baseball.

QUIZ: True or false? Pull-Yer-Leg is the only horse to win the Kentucky Derby twice.

Trivia Timeout
The average pro football player's career is three years.

QUIZ ANSWER: False. Since the Kentucky Derby is only for three-year-old's, it is impossible to compete twice.

APRIL 16th

TODAY'S THOUGHT: "It's not whether you win or lose, but who gets the blame." —*Blaine Nye, former Dallas Cowboy*

HISTORY: On this date in 1987 Michael Jordan put on a spectacular exhibition in a losing cause. Jordan scored 61 points — including a record 23 in a row — but the Bulls fell to the Hawks, 117-114.

QUIZ: Four NFL running backs have gained over 2,000 yards in a season. How many can you name?

Trivia Timeout
Hockey is called "shinny" in Scotland.

QUIZ ANSWER: Terrell Davis, Barry Sanders, Eric Dickerson and O.J. Simpson

APRIL 17th

TODAY'S THOUGHT: "Let him hit it — you got fielders behind you."
—*Alexander Cartwright, baseball founding father*

HISTORY: On this date in 1976 Mike Schmidt's four consecutive home runs turned a 13-2 Cubs' lead into an 18-16 Phillies' win. The last of Schmidt's homers was the game-winner in the 10th inning.

QUIZ: Who was the basketball coach who replaced the legendary John Wooden at UCLA?

Trivia Timeout

Keith Jackson, Howard Cosell and Don Meredith were the first announcers on ABC's "Monday Night Football".

QUIZ ANSWER: Gene Bartow

APRIL 18th

TODAY'S THOUGHT: "Baseball is like church. Many attend. Few understand." —*Leo Durocher*

HISTORY: On this date in 1923 Babe Ruth christened the "House That Ruth Built" with a three-run home run. A crowd of 74,200 attended the first game ever played in Yankee Stadium, a 4-1 triumph over the Red Sox.

QUIZ: Who was the first player to lead the NBA in scoring and assists in the same season?

Trivia Timeout

Scott and Brennan Olson invented Rollerblades in 1980.

QUIZ ANSWER: Nate Archibald scored 34 points per game and handed out 11.4 assists for the Kansas City Kings in the 1972-73 season.

APRIL 19th

TODAY'S THOUGHT: "I get my exercise running to the funerals of my friends who exercise." —*Barry Gray*

HISTORY: On this date in 1897 fifteen runners competed in the first Boston Marathon. New Yorker John J. McDermott crossed the finish line in 2:55:10 to win the race. Five of the competitors dropped out.

QUIZ: Whose statue stands outside the Pro Football Hall of Fame in Canton, Ohio?

Trivia Timeout
The course for the first Boston Marathon was only 24-1/2 miles long versus the official distance of 26 miles, 385 yards.

QUIZ ANSWER: Jim Thorpe

APRIL 20th

TODAY'S THOUGHT: "Fishing: The art of taking more fish out of a stream than were ever in it."
—*Oliver Herford*

HISTORY: On this date in 1982 the Braves beat the Reds, 4-2, raising their record to 12-0 — the best start in Major League history. Proving that it's not how you start but how you finish, Atlanta ended the season in third place.

QUIZ: How many men defeated Muhammad Ali?

Trivia Timeout
Ping pong is the national sport of China.

QUIZ ANSWER: Five: Trevor Berbick, Joe Frazier, Larry Holmes, Ken Norton and Leon Spinks

APRIL 21st

TODAY'S THOUGHT: "The older they get, the better they were when they were younger." —*Jim Bouton*

HISTORY: On this date in 1977 Moses Malone set a record for the most offensive rebounds in a play-off game, pulling down 15 in Houston's win against Washington.

QUIZ: Can you name the three NBA teams that Bill Russell coached in his career?

Trivia Timeout

Martina Navratilova was born as Martina Subertova. When her mother later divorced and remarried, the tennis superstar took the name of her stepfather, Miroslav Navratil, adding the traditional feminine ending "ova".

QUIZ ANSWER: Russell was head coach of the Boston Celtics, Seattle Supersonics and the Sacramento Kings.

APRIL 22nd

TODAY'S THOUGHT: "Blind people come to the park just to listen to him pitch."
—*Reggie Jackson, on Tom Seaver*

HISTORY: On this date in 1970 Tom Seaver tied a then Major League record by striking out 19 Padres in a game. Seaver fanned the last 10 batters that he faced to set still another mark, in the Mets' 2-1 win.

QUIZ: Three men have become NFL head coaches before their 35th birthdays. Two of them are named Shula — Don and David. Who's the third?

Trivia Timeout

The "stuff" that umpires rub down baseballs with before each game is called Baltimore Clay.

QUIZ ANSWER: John Madden

APRIL 23rd

TODAY'S THOUGHT: "Hitting is timing. Pitching is upsetting timing." —*Warren Spahn*

HISTORY: On this date in 1950 the Minneapolis Lakers won the first NBA championship besting the Syracuse Nationals.

QUIZ: True or false? Tennis great Rod Laver is the only man to win the Grand Slam twice.

Trivia Timeout

Hall of Fame pitcher Warren Spahn's career lasted long enough to play under manager Casey Stengel both "before and after (Stengel) was a genuis" — as he put it. Spahn encountered Stengel in 1942 with the Boston Braves and in 1965 with the Mets.

QUIZ ANSWER: True, in 1962 and 1969

APRIL 24th

TODAY'S THOUGHT: "Football doesn't build character. It eliminates weak ones." —*Darrell Royal, former coach*

HISTORY: On this date in 1967 the Philadelphia 76ers beat San Francisco, 125-122, to capture the NBA title in six games. It marked the first time in nine years that the Boston Celtics had not won the championship.

QUIZ: Three Dodgers shared the MVP award in the 1981 World Series. Name them.

Trivia Timeout

Bill Singer is the pitcher credited with baseball's first save. The statistic made its debut in 1969 when Singer was playing with the Dodgers.

QUIZ ANSWER: Pedro Guerrero, Ron Cey and Steve Yeager were the MVP trio.

APRIL 25th

TODAY'S THOUGHT: "I always turn to the sports pages first, which record people's accomplishments. The front page has nothing but man's failures."
—*Chief Justice Earl Warren*

HISTORY: On this date in 1974 the NFL adopted sudden-death overtime for the regular season. If no team scores in the extra 15-minute period, the game ends in a tie.

QUIZ: Including both the city and team, which two letters are not used in spelling the name of any of the NFL clubs?

Trivia Timeout
The shape of a football is a prolate spheroid.

QUIZ ANSWER: Q and X

APRIL 26th

TODAY'S THOUGHT: "Baseball: An island of surety in a changing world." —*Bill Veeck*

HISTORY: On this date in 1961 Yankees outfielder Roger Maris hit his first home run of the season in the team's 11th game of the year. Maris picked up the pace though, hitting 60 more to break Babe Ruth's record.

QUIZ: What pitcher gave up the first of Roger Maris' 61 homers in 1961?

Trivia Timeout
In the 1912 Shawnee Invitational for Ladies at Shawnee-on-Delaware, PA a contestant recorded a well-over-par 166 on the 16th-hole. After playing the shot from a rowboat, she finally managed to sink the floating ball in the cup.

QUIZ ANSWER: Paul Foytack

APRIL 27th

TODAY'S THOUGHT: "Every man's got to figure to get beat sometime." —*Joe Louis*

HISTORY: On this date in 1956 Rocky Marciano retired. Marciano remains the only heavyweight champ to retire with a perfect record, 49-0.

QUIZ: George Gervin needed 58 points in the final game of the 1977-78 season to win the NBA scoring title. Gervin scored 63 points to finish first with a 27.21 point average. Whom did Gervin edge out for the title?

Trivia Timeout
Patrick Ewing was the first pick ever in the NBA lottery.

QUIZ ANSWER: David Thompson of the Denver Nuggets who, despite scoring 73 points in the final game, fell short with an average of 27.15 points

APRIL 28th

TODAY'S THOUGHT: "A champion is afraid of losing; everyone else is afraid of winning." —*Billie Jean King*

HISTORY: On this date in 1966 the Boston Celtics won their seventh consecutive NBA title, beating the Los Angeles Lakers, 95-93. Celtics coach Red Auerbach resigned after the game to become the team's GM.

QUIZ: In the NFL, how many players may a team have on its active roster?

Trivia Timeout
Florence Griffith Joyner holds the world record for the women's 100-meter run at 10.49 seconds. At the 1956 Olympic Games, that would have been good enough for the gold — in the men's event.

QUIZ ANSWER: 45

APRIL 29th

TODAY'S THOUGHT: "Never trust a base runner who's limping. Come a base hit and you'll think he just got back from Lourdes." —*Joe Garagiola*

HISTORY: On this date in 1986 Roger Clemens set a new Major League record for strikeouts in a nine-inning game. The Bosox right-hander whiffed 20 batters, including eight in a row, in a win over Seattle.

QUIZ: What player did Andre Agassi defeat to win his first Wimbledon title in 1992?

Trivia Timeout

Clemens is the only player to have been the MVP, the Cy Young Award winner and the All-Star Game MVP in the same year — all in 1986.

QUIZ ANSWER: Goran Ivanisevic

APRIL 30th

TODAY'S THOUGHT: "Today, I consider myself the luckiest man on the face of the earth."
—*Lou Gehrig, in his retirement speech, delivered before a sellout crowd at Yankee Stadium*

HISTORY: On this date in 1939 Lou Gehrig played in his 2,130th consecutive game, the last in his career. Amyotrophic lateral sclerosis not only brought an end to his streak but claimed his life two years later.

QUIZ: Who was the first Dallas Cowboy to rush for 1,000 yards in a single season?

Trivia Timeout

Golf balls were originally made of leather and stuffed with goose feathers.

QUIZ ANSWER: Calvin Hill

MAY 1st

TODAY'S THOUGHT: "A woman who has never seen her husband fishing doesn't know what a patient man she's married." —*Ed Howe*

HISTORY: On this date in 1991 44-year old Nolan Ryan threw the seventh no-hitter of his career, his sixth in the American League. Ryan fanned 16 as he shut down Toronto, 3-0.

QUIZ: Name the horse that Steve Cauthen rode to the Triple Crown in 1978.

Trivia Timeout

Despite winning 324 games and striking out 5,714 batters, Nolan Ryan never won the Cy Young Award.

QUIZ ANSWER: Cauthen rode Affirmed to the Triple Crown.

MAY 2nd

TODAY'S THOUGHT: "Being a sports fan is a complex matter, in part irrational...but not unworthy...a relief from the seriousness of the real world, with its unending pressures and often grave obligations." —*Richard Gilmam*

HISTORY: On this date in 1967 the underdog Toronto Maple Leafs beat the Montreal Canadiens, 3-1, to take home the Stanley Cup.

QUIZ: True or false? Any player who shatters the backboard in a NBA game is automatically ejected.

Trivia Timeout

Jimmy Carter was the first president to attend a "Monday Night Football" game.

QUIZ ANSWER: False. A technical foul is given.

MAY 3rd

TODAY'S THOUGHT: "Rail-splitting produced an immortal president in Lincoln, but golf hasn't produced even a good A-1 congressman." —*Will Rogers*

HISTORY: On this date in 1952 Eddie Arcaro rode Hill Gail to victory in the Kentucky Derby. Arcaro also rode into the record books, becoming the first jockey to win the "Run for the Roses" five times.

QUIZ: Cy Young is the pitcher with the most career victories in the Major Leagues, 511. Who is number two on the list?

Trivia Timeout

The emblem on the New Orleans Saints helmets is a fleur-de-lis.

QUIZ ANSWER: Walter Johnson, with 416

MAY 4th

TODAY'S THOUGHT: " 'How you play the game' is for college boys. When you're playing for money, winning is the only thing that counts." —*Leo Durocher*

HISTORY: On this date in 1957 jockey Willie Shoemaker misjudged the finish line at Churchill Downs, allowing Iron Liege to pass him and take the Kentucky Derby.

QUIZ: Which team won the first American Basketball Association championship?

Trivia Timeout

Brokers Tip won only one race in his career — the 1933 Kentucky Derby.

QUIZ ANSWER: The Pittsburgh Pipers

MAY 5th

TODAY'S THOUGHT: "Most ball games are lost, not won." —*Casey Stengel*

HISTORY: On this date in 1969, for the seventh time in 11 years, the LA Lakers lost the NBA championship series to the Celtics.

QUIZ: During the 1950's, all ten American League pennants were won by teams managed by these two men. Who are they?

Trivia Timeout
Jerry West was the model for the NBA's silhouette logo.

QUIZ ANSWER: Al Lopez managed Cleveland to the pennant in 1954 and Chicago in 1959. The other eight were won by the Yankees and skipper Casey Stengel.

MAY 6th

TODAY'S THOUGHT: "Snider, Mantle and Mays — you could get a fat lip in any saloon by starting an argument as to which was best. One point was beyond argument, though. Willie was by all odds the most exciting." —*Red Smith*

HISTORY: On this date in 1954 Roger Bannister became the first man to run the mile in less than four minutes. The British student broke the tape in 3:59.4.

QUIZ: Where are the Cotton, Rose, Orange and Sugar Bowls played?

Trivia Timeout
Pro football coach Bill Parcells' real first name is Duane.

QUIZ ANSWER: Dallas, TX; Pasadena, CA; Miami, FL and New Orleans, LA

MAY 7th

TODAY'S THOUGHT: "It's what you learn after you know it all that counts." —*John Wooden*

HISTORY: On this date in 1972 after losing in eight NBA championship finals, the Lakers finally won one. Los Angeles beat the New York Knicks, 114-100, to take the series, four games to one.

QUIZ: What NBA franchise was originally known as the Buffalo Braves?

Trivia Timeout
Johnny Unitas was named "The Sporting News" NFL Player of the Year three times.

QUIZ ANSWER: The Braves moved to San Diego and changed the team name to the Clippers. The Clippers finally set sail for Los Angeles, keeping the name.

MAY 8th

TODAY'S THOUGHT: "To be a great champion, you must believe you are the best. If you're not, pretend you are." —*Muhammad Ali*

HISTORY: On this date in 1953 shot-putter Parry O'Brien became the first man to hurl the 16-pound shot 60 feet with a throw of 60 feet, 5-1/4 inches. Exactly 11 years to the day later, Randy Matson cracked the 70 foot barrier with a toss of 70 feet, 7 inches.

QUIZ: What Major League baseball team has the dubious distinction of finishing a season with 120 losses?

Trivia Timeout
Hall of Fame pitchers Bob Gibson and Ferguson Jenkins both played for the Harlem Globetrotters.

QUIZ ANSWER: The not-so-amazin' 1962 Mets

MAY 9th

TODAY'S THOUGHT: "Golf does strange things to other people, too. It makes liars out of honest men, cheats out of altruists, cowards out of brave men and fools out of everybody." —*Milton Gross*

HISTORY: On this date in 1961 Baltimore Orioles first baseman Jim Gentile set a Major League record, hitting grand slam homers in consecutive at bats.

QUIZ: What college has won the most Division I NCAA golf championships?

Trivia Timeout
Pat LaFontaine holds the NHL record for the quickest two goals at the beginning of a period — 35 seconds.

QUIZ ANSWER: Yale

MAY 10th

TODAY'S THOUGHT: "I skate to where the puck is going to be, not where it has been." —*Wayne Gretzky*

HISTORY: On this date in 1970 Bobby Orr's overtime goal gave the Boston Bruins a 4-3 win and a sweep of the St. Louis Blues in the Stanley Cup finals. It was the first NHL championship in 29 years for the Bruins.

QUIZ: Who is the only tennis player to win seven singles titles at the French Open?

Trivia Timeout
The Bruins purchased the rights to Bobby Orr when he was just 14 years old.

QUIZ ANSWER: Chris Evert, who won in 1974, '75, '79, '80, '83, '85 and '86

MAY 11th

TODAY'S THOUGHT: "You're expected to be perfect the day you start, and then improve."
—Ed Vargo, supervisor of umpires

HISTORY: On this date in 1971 Cleveland pitcher Steve Dunning hit a grand slam against Oakland, the last AL pitcher to accomplish this feat.

QUIZ: Who is the only man to hit 50 home runs in a season more than once and yet retire with fewer than 500 lifetime homers?

Trivia Timeout

A doubles tennis court is nine feet wider than a singles playing surface.

QUIZ ANSWER: Ralph Kiner hit 51 homers in 1947 and 54 in 1949. He finished his career with 369.

MAY 12th

TODAY'S THOUGHT: "If you don't know where you're going, you could wind up someplace else." *—Yogi Berra*

HISTORY: On this date in 1982 the United States Football League was founded. Twelve teams competed in the spring league, which folded four years later despite avoiding head-to-head competition with the NFL.

QUIZ: What is NBA coaching legend Red Auerbach's real first name?

Trivia Timeout

When he was chasing the Babe's career home run record, Henry Aaron often avoided attention by registering at hotels under the alias George Ruth.

QUIZ ANSWER: Arnold

The Bathroom Sports Almanac

MAY 13th

TODAY'S THOUGHT: "He's just telling us, 'They're number one.' " —*Don Meredith, acknowledging an obscene gesture by a fan on "Monday Night Football"*

HISTORY: On this date in 1976 the New Jersey Nets defeated the Denver Nuggets, 112-106, to win the last American Basketball Association title.

QUIZ: Who were the opponents in the first game of ABC's "Monday Night Football"?

Trivia Timeout
Former pitcher Tommy John's doorbell plays "Take Me Out to the Ball Game".

QUIZ ANSWER: The Browns beat the Jets, 31-21, in the first "Monday Night" game in 1970.

MAY 14th

TODAY'S THOUGHT: "If it is true that a sports career prolongs adolescence, it is also true that when that career ends, it deposits a player into premature middle age." —*Ken Dryden*

HISTORY: On this date in 1966 Bob Seagren broke the indoor pole vault record, clearing 17 feet, 5-1/4 inches. It was the first of five times that Seagren set the mark.

QUIZ: From 1988 to 1990 the NL RBI crown was worn by three members of the Giants. Name this trio.

Trivia Timeout
Baseball player Gary Sheffield had his initials inlaid with gold on his front teeth.

QUIZ ANSWER: Will Clark, Kevin Mitchell and Matt Williams were the respective leaders in those years.

MAY 15th

TODAY'S THOUGHT: "George Brett could roll out of bed on Christmas morning and hit a line drive."
—John Schuerholtz, Royals GM

HISTORY: On this date in 1973 Nolan Ryan threw the first of seven career no-hitters as the California Angels shut down Kansas City, 3-0.

QUIZ: Right-hander Nolan Ryan leads all pitchers with 5,714 career strikeouts. What pitcher has the most strikeouts for left-handers?

Trivia Timeout

Andre Agassi is a right-handed tennis player but he swings a golf club lefty.

QUIZ ANSWER: Steve Carlton is the leading lefty strikeout artist. Carlton retired with 4,136 K's.

MAY 16th

TODAY'S THOUGHT: "Some people have a chip on their shoulder. Billy has a whole lumberyard."
—Jim Murray, on Billy Martin

HISTORY: On this date in 1980 Magic Johnson, filling in at center for the injured Kareem Adbul-Jabbar, scored 42 points and grabbed 15 rebounds, leading the Lakers to a 123-107 win over Philadelphia.

QUIZ: True or false? The Big 10 once prohibited live television broadcasts of its football games.

Trivia Timeout

New York's Polo Grounds hosted baseball, football and even boxing — but never a polo match.

QUIZ ANSWER: True. The conference banned same-day TV in 1950.

MAY 17th

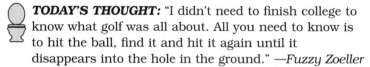

TODAY'S THOUGHT: "I didn't need to finish college to know what golf was all about. All you need to know is to hit the ball, find it and hit it again until it disappears into the hole in the ground." —*Fuzzy Zoeller*

HISTORY: On this date in 1875 fifteen horses ran in the first Kentucky Derby. The winner was Aristedes.

QUIZ: Three fillies have won the Kentucky Derby. Regret did it in 1915, while Genuine Risk led the field in 1980. What filly won most recently and when?

Trivia Timeout

The symbol "K" used to signify a strikeout comes from the last letter of the word "struck".

QUIZ ANSWER: Winning Colors, in 1988

MAY 18th

TODAY'S THOUGHT: "A team is where a boy can prove courage on his own. A gang is where a coward goes to hide." —*Mickey Mantle*

HISTORY: On this date in 1957 jockey Eddie Arcaro guided Bold Ruler to an easy two-length win in the Preakness. For Arcaro, it was the sixth and final Preakness win of his long career.

QUIZ: Only two players have hit three home runs in a single World Series game. You may recall Reggie Jackson did it in 1977. Who is the other slugger?

Trivia Timeout

Man O' War lost only one race — to a horse named Upset.

QUIZ ANSWER: Babe Ruth, who did it twice in the 20's

MAY 19th

TODAY'S THOUGHT: "The charm of fishing is that it is the pursuit of what is elusive but obtainable..."
—John Buchan

HISTORY: On this date in 1974 goalie Bernie Parent led Philadelphia to a 1-0 victory over Boston to give the Flyers their first Stanley Cup. The Flyers had entered the NHL as an expansion team just seven years earlier.

QUIZ: When Bill Laimbeer won the NBA rebounding title in the 1985-86 season, he snapped another player's string of five straight titles. Who was it?

Trivia Timeout
Pitcher Roger Clemens doesn't shave on the day of a scheduled start.

QUIZ ANSWER: Moses Malone

MAY 20th

TODAY'S THOUGHT: "I wanted to be like Nolan Ryan. I didn't want to be like Pete Gray." *—Jim Abbott*

HISTORY: On this date in 1945 lead-off hitter Pete Gray drove in two runs with three hits as the St. Louis Browns beat the Yankees, 10-1. Gray was a leftfielder...a one-armed leftfielder.

QUIZ: Where did Jim Abbott play his college ball?

Trivia Timeout
Rap singer Hammer was a batboy for the Oakland A's.

QUIZ ANSWER: Abbott pitched for the Michigan Wolverines.

MAY 21st

TODAY'S THOUGHT: "When you play for fun, it's fun. But when you play golf for a living, it's a game of sorrows. You're never happy." —*Gary Player*

HISTORY: On this date in 1977 Seattle Slew beat Iron Constitution to take the Preakness Stakes.

QUIZ: In 1974 this school snapped UCLA's streak of seven consecutive college basketball national championships when it bested the Bruins in the semifinals. Who was it?

Trivia Timeout

Basketballer Jamal Mashburn's father was a heavyweight boxer who fought Larry Holmes and Ken Norton.

QUIZ ANSWER: North Carolina State, who went on to beat Marquette in the finals

MAY 22nd

TODAY'S THOUGHT: "On the day of the race, a lot of people want you to sign something just before you get in the car so that they can say they got your last autograph." —*A.J. Foyt*

HISTORY: On this date in 1977 Janet Guthrie became the first woman to qualify for the Indianapolis 500.

QUIZ: Who is considered the first soccer-style kicker to play pro football?

Trivia Timeout

According to Metropolitan Life, baseball players live significantly longer than the average male — especially third basemen.

QUIZ ANSWER: Pete Gogolak

MAY 23rd

TODAY'S THOUGHT: "It's not whether you get knocked down. It's whether you get up again."
—*Vince Lombardi*

HISTORY: On this date in 1922 boxer Gene Tunney suffered the only defeat of his career. Tunney was decisioned by Harry Greb in a light-heavyweight championship bout. Tunney avenged the defeat before moving up to heavyweight and winning that crown.

QUIZ: What high school did Kareem Abdul-Jabbar attend?

Trivia Timeout
Former fighter Marvin Hagler relaxes by raising pigeons.

QUIZ ANSWER: Kareem (then Lew Alcindor) attended Manhattan's Power Memorial.

MAY 24th

TODAY'S THOUGHT: "Will the last person to leave the stadium please turn out the lights." —*Banner at Wrigley Field after lights were installed in 1988*

HISTORY: On this date in 1935 President Franklin Delano Roosevelt pressed a button at the White House that turned on the lights at Cincinnati's Crosley Field for Major League baseball's first night game.

QUIZ: Who was the youngest player to throw a World Series shutout?

Trivia Timeout
Jockey Laffit Pincay, Jr. has to maintain a 600 calorie a day diet to keep his weight down.

QUIZ ANSWER: Jim Palmer of the Orioles, who at age 20 spoiled Sandy Koufax's career finale in 1966

MAY 25th

TODAY'S THOUGHT: "Sports is like a war without the killing." —*Ted Turner*

HISTORY: On this date in 1965 Muhammad Ali (nee Cassius Clay) knocked out Sonny Liston in the first round of their championship rematch. Fewer than 3,000 fans attended the bout held in Lewiston, Maine.

QUIZ: Who is the NFL's all-time career leader in rushing?

Trivia Timeout
People wonder who was more embarrassed that night in Maine, Liston or Robert Goulet. The Canadian-born singer forgot the words to the "Star Spangled Banner" while singing before the fight.

QUIZ ANSWER: Walter Payton of the Chicago Bears, who ran for 16,726 yards in his 13-year career

MAY 26th

TODAY'S THOUGHT: "Becoming number one is easier than remaining number one." —*Bill Bradley*

HISTORY: On this date in 1959 Pirates pitcher Harvey Haddix was perfect for 12 innings, but an error, an intentional walk and a double allowed the Braves to get by the Pirates and Haddix, 1-0, in 13 innings.

QUIZ: The U.S. Olympic hockey team has won the gold twice. You probably recall Lake Placid in 1980. Where and when was its other gold medal performance?

Trivia Timeout
Tennis was originally called "sphairistike" which in Greek means "to play".

QUIZ ANSWER: The U.S. team's previous gold medal was earned at Squaw Valley in 1960.

MAY 27th

TODAY'S THOUGHT: "Managing is getting paid for home runs someone else hits." —*Casey Stengel*

HISTORY: On this date in 1985 Kentucky Derby winner Spend A Buck made a buck and then some, winning the largest purse in horse racing history, $2.6 million.

QUIZ: Gavvy Cravath of Philadelphia led the National League in home runs six times. Can you name the three other sluggers who have equaled this feat?

Trivia Timeout

Michael Jordan's license plate reads "JUMP23".

QUIZ ANSWER: Mel Ott, six times; Ralph Kiner, seven; and Mike Schmidt, eight

MAY 28th

TODAY'S THOUGHT: "Luck is the residue of design." —*Branch Rickey*

HISTORY: On this date in 1956 Pirates first baseman Dale Long became the first player to homer in eight straight games.

QUIZ: Jack Nicklaus is one of four golfers to have won the Masters, the U.S. Open, the British Open and the PGA Championship. Who are the other three?

Trivia Timeout

In 1908 Hall of Fame pitcher Walter Johnson pitched three shutouts in four days, allowing a grand total of just twelve hits.

QUIZ ANSWER: Ben Hogan, Gene Sarazen and Gary Player

MAY 29th

TODAY'S THOUGHT: "That's as true as I can tell you. There are things in there that I'd never want to come out in public." —*George Steinbrenner, to Fay Vincent*

HISTORY: On this date in 1990 Rickey Henderson of the Oakland A's passed Ty Cobb as the American League's all-time stolen base leader, swiping #893.

QUIZ: Name the baseball Hall of Famer who was Rookie of the Year in 1959 despite playing in only 59 games.

Trivia Timeout

Best-selling baby book author Dr. Benjamin Spock won a gold medal in rowing in the 1924 Olympics.

QUIZ ANSWER: San Francisco Giants first baseman Willie McCovey hit .354 with 13 home runs and 38 RBI's to earn the award.

MAY 30th

TODAY'S THOUGHT: "You don't do things right once in a while. You do them right all the time."
—*Vince Lombardi*

HISTORY: On this date in 1966 nearly half of the thirty-three car field was wiped out in a first lap crash at the Indianapolis Motor Speedway. Miraculously, only one driver was injured.

QUIZ: Can you name the only team to beat Vince Lombardi in an NFL postseason game?

Trivia Timeout

The Olympic flame was conceived for the Games by none other than Adolf Hitler.

QUIZ ANSWER: The Philadelphia Eagles, who defeated Lombardi's Packers in the 1960 NFL championship

The Bathroom Sports Almanac

MAY 31st

 TODAY'S THOUGHT: "I like my girls blonde and my Johnny Walker Red." —*Joe Namath*

HISTORY: On this date in 1983 Moses Malone led the Philadelphia 76ers to a 115-108 win over the Los Angeles Lakers and a four-game sweep of the championship series.

QUIZ: Who is the only baseball Hall of Famer whose last name begins with the letter "I"?

Trivia Timeout

Moses Malone never played college basketball. He went right from Petersburg (VA) High School to the ABA's Utah Stars in 1974.

QUIZ ANSWER: Monte Irvin, who played with the Giants and the Cubs, entered Cooperstown in 1973.

JUNE 1st

TODAY'S THOUGHT: "A golf course is the epitome of all that is transitory in the universe, a space not to dwell in, but to get over as quickly as possible."
—*Jean Giraudoux*

HISTORY: On this date in 1971 Nolan Ryan notched his 100th career victory in grand style, pitching his fourth career no-hitter.

QUIZ: Who scored the winning touchdown in Baltimore's 23-17 overtime win against the Giants in the 1958 championship game?

Trivia Timeout

In the opening march of the Olympics, Greece always leads the parade and the host country is last.

QUIZ ANSWER: Running back Alan Ameche

JUNE 2nd

TODAY'S THOUGHT: "I swam my brains out."
—*Mark Spitz, on the record seven gold medals he won in the 1972 Olympics*

HISTORY: On this date in 1935 the playing career of Babe Ruth came to an end. The Boston Braves gave the 41-year old slugger his unconditional release.

QUIZ: Heavyweight champion Joe Louis lost only three fights in his 17-year pro career. Can you name the trio who downed the "Brown Bomber"?

Trivia Timeout

Actor Johnny Weissmuller monkeyed around as Tarzan but he was a serious swimmer with five Olympic gold medals.

QUIZ ANSWER: Max Schmeling in 1936; Ezzard Charles in 1950; and Rocky Marciano in 1951

JUNE 3rd

TODAY'S THOUGHT: "Why they call a fellow that keeps losing all the time a good sport gets me."
—*Kin Hubbard*

HISTORY: On this date in 1932 Lou Gehrig became the first Major Leaguer to hit four consecutive home runs in a game.

QUIZ: Name the last Ivy League basketball team to make it to the NCAA Final Four.

Trivia Timeout
Clyde Van Dusen, the winner of the 1929 Kentucky Derby, was named after his trainer.

QUIZ ANSWER: The University of Pennsylvania, who lost to Magic Johnson and Michigan State in the semifinal game, 101-67, in 1979

JUNE 4th

TODAY'S THOUGHT: "A muscle is like a car. If you want it to run well early in the morning, you have to warm it up." —*Florence Griffith-Joyner*

HISTORY: On this date in 1987 track and field's longest winning streak came to a stumbling end. Edwin Moses clipped the final hurdle in the 400 meters, allowing fellow American Danny Harris to cross the finish line just ahead of him. Moses had won 122 straight races over almost 10 years.

QUIZ: Only one Major Leaguer has won a batting title in three different decades. Who?

Trivia Timeout
A hockey puck is 3" in diameter.

QUIZ ANSWER: George Brett, in 1976, 1980 and 1990

JUNE 5th

TODAY'S THOUGHT: "Nothing improves a fisherman's luck like fish in a biting mood." —*Catfish Moore*

HISTORY: On this date in 1977 the Portland Trail Blazers beat the Philadelphia 76ers, 109-107, to win their first NBA title.

QUIZ: Who is the only man to play in the NBA finals and coach in the Super Bowl?

Trivia Timeout
The last time that both men's singles finalists at Wimbledon were left-handed was in 1984 when John McEnroe bested Jimmy Connors.

QUIZ ANSWER: Bud Grant was a reserve forward on the 1949-50 NBA champion Minneapolis Lakers. Grant later coached the Minnesota Vikings to four Super Bowls.

JUNE 6th

TODAY'S THOUGHT: "Some people are so busy learning the tricks of the trade that they never learn the trade." —*Vernon Law, Pittsburgh Pirates pitcher*

HISTORY: On this date in 1892 Benjamin Harrison became the first president to attend a Major League baseball game.

QUIZ: How many NFL teams have bird nicknames?

Trivia Timeout
Hockey superstar Wayne Gretzky was presented with a Rolls-Royce when he scored his 802nd goal, passing Gordie Howe to become the NHL's all-time leader. The license plate ... "GOAL802".

QUIZ ANSWER: Five - Atlanta Falcons, Arizona Cardinals, Baltimore Ravens, Philadelphia Eagles and Seattle Seahawks

JUNE 7th

TODAY'S THOUGHT: "I love baseball. It's given me everything I have. Look, there are only about 600 Major Leaguers in the country. You have to feel special." —*Thurman Munson*

HISTORY: On this date in 1941 Whirlaway won the Belmont Stakes by two and a half lengths. This victory marked the first of two Triple Crowns collected by jockey Eddie Arcaro in his career.

QUIZ: Can you recall the last National League pitcher to win the MVP award?

Trivia Timeout
Boxer Rocky Graziano was once TV talk show host Merv Griffin's on-air sidekick.

QUIZ ANSWER: Bob Gibson of the Cardinals in 1968

JUNE 8th

TODAY'S THOUGHT: "A life isn't significant except for its impact on other lives." —*Jackie Robinson*

HISTORY: On this date in 1966 the battle between the AFL and NFL came to an end with the announcement of the merger of the leagues.

QUIZ: In 1980 the Boston Celtics traded the top pick in the draft to Golden State for Robert Parish and the third overall selection. Whom did Boston choose with that pick?

Trivia Timeout
Football's San Diego Chargers were, believe it or not, named after charge cards. Their first owner, Barron Hilton, was known as the Carte Blanche baron.

QUIZ ANSWER: Kevin McHale

JUNE 9th

TODAY'S THOUGHT: "If God had meant for Wimbledon to be played in great weather, he would have put it in Acapulco." —*Anonymous*

HISTORY: On this date in 1984 Martina Navratilova defeated Chris Evert Lloyd, 7-6, 6-2 to win her third straight Wimbledon Championship.

QUIZ: Who was the only NHL defenseman to win an NHL scoring title?

Trivia Timeout
That same year, Navratilova won three of the four Grand Slam events. The only event that eluded her was the Australian Open.

QUIZ ANSWER: Bobby Orr, of the Boston Bruins — Orr won the title twice, in 1970 and '75.

JUNE 10th

TODAY'S THOUGHT: "Football: A sport that bears the same relation to education that bullfighting does to agriculture." —*Elbert Hubbard*

HISTORY: On this date in 1978 it was Affirmed by a head over Alydar in the Belmont, giving horse racing back-to-back Triple Crown winners for the first time in history. Seattle Slew had captured the Crown in 1977.

QUIZ: Which sport has had more Triple Crown winners, horse racing or Major League baseball?

Trivia Timeout
Alydar finished second to Affirmed in the Kentucky Derby and the Preakness Stakes as well as at Belmont.

QUIZ ANSWER: There have been 11 Triple Crown winners both at the track and on the diamond.

JUNE 11th

TODAY'S THOUGHT: "The difference between a successful person and others is not a lack of strength, not a lack of knowledge, but a lack of will."
—*Vince Lombardi*

HISTORY: On this date in 1967 the wind was blowing out at Wrigley Field when the Cubs and Mets tied a Major League record with 11 home runs between them. The Cubs — with seven homers — prevailed, 18-10.

QUIZ: Name the switch-hitter with the most career hits.

Trivia Timeout

Joe Montana is from Eagle Pass, Pennsylvania but his namesake town lies much further west...Joe, Montana.

QUIZ ANSWER: Switch-hitter Pete Rose finished his career with 4,256 hits.

JUNE 12th

TODAY'S THOUGHT: "I'd rather be lucky than good."
—*Lefty Gomez*

HISTORY: On this date in 1991 the Chicago Bulls beat the Los Angeles Lakers, 108-101, to win the NBA title in five games. Series MVP Michael Jordan led the way with 30 points.

QUIZ: When an NFL official drops a flag, it's bright gold. What color were the penalty flags until 1965?

Trivia Timeout

The first black man drafted by an NBA team was Chuck Cooper of the Boston Celtics.

QUIZ ANSWER: White

JUNE 13th

TODAY'S THOUGHT: "If there is any larceny in a man, golf will bring it out." —*Paul Gallico*

HISTORY: On this date in 1953 golfer Ben Hogan finished six strokes ahead of Sam Snead to win his record-tying fourth U.S. Open.

QUIZ: Four Major Leaguers have stolen 100 or more bases in a season. Rickey Henderson and Vince Coleman are the most recent. Who are the other two?

Trivia Timeout
Red Grange's given name is "Harold".

QUIZ ANSWER: Maury Wills stole 104 bases in 1962 and Lou Brock pilfered 118 in 1974. Henderson and Coleman have topped the century mark three times apiece — all in the 1980's.

JUNE 14th

TODAY'S THOUGHT: "Cardinal rule for all hitters with two strikes on them: Never trust the umpire!"
—*Robert Smith*

HISTORY: On this date in 1994 the curse was broken as the New York Rangers won the Stanley Cup for the first time since 1940. New York beat Vancouver, 3-2, in game seven of the NHL finals.

QUIZ: In golf, what is a stymie?

Trivia Timeout
The Rangers' Brian Leetch, the Conn Smythe Trophy winner as the 1994 play-off MVP, was the first U.S.-born player to receive this award in the history of the NHL.

QUIZ ANSWER: An intentional illegal putt to place the ball between the opponent's ball and the cup

JUNE 15th

TODAY'S THOUGHT: "There is no chance night baseball ever will become popular." —*Clark Griffith*

HISTORY: On this date in 1938 Cincinnati's Johnny Vander Meer threw his second straight no-hitter, shutting out the Dodgers, 6-0. Four days earlier, Vander Meer had no-hit the Boston Braves, 3-0.

QUIZ: Can you name the only center — other than Wilt Chamberlain — to win the NBA's Rookie of the Year and MVP awards in the same season?

Trivia Timeout

The Reds-Dodgers game was notable for another reason: It was the first night game played at Ebbets Field.

QUIZ ANSWER: Wes Unseld of the Baltimore Bullets

JUNE 16th

TODAY'S THOUGHT: "No mas!" —*Roberto Duran, in his abbreviated fight against Sugar Ray Leonard*

HISTORY: On this date in 1975 the Milwaukee Bucks traded Kareem Abdul-Jabbar to the Los Angeles Lakers for center Elmore Smith and guards Brian Winters, Dave Meyers and Junior Bridgeman.

QUIZ: What Cub was the first player to win the MVP award while playing for a last-place team?

Trivia Timeout

In Abdul-Jabbar's final year in Milwaukee, the Bucks finished the season 38-44. The year after the trade, the Bucks' record was...38-44.

QUIZ ANSWER: Andre Dawson, who was MVP in 1987 — Dawson hit .287 with 49 home runs and 137 RBI's.

JUNE 17th

TODAY'S THOUGHT: "You have to take your job seriously, but you can't take yourself seriously."
—*Brent Musburger*

HISTORY: On this date in 1960 Boston Red Sox slugger Ted Williams hit the 500th home run of his career.

QUIZ: Who was the last man to score six touchdowns in an NFL game?

Trivia Timeout
The Los Angeles Rams were the first NFL players to have emblems on their helmets. Running back Fred Gehrke, an art major in college, painted horns on their headgear in 1948.

QUIZ ANSWER: Gale Sayers had a half dozen TD's against the 49ers in 1965.

JUNE 18th

TODAY'S THOUGHT: "Putting is not golf but croquet."
—*A.A. Milne*

HISTORY: On this date in 1960 Arnold Palmer rallied from a seven-stroke deficit at the start of the final round to win his first U.S. Open. Palmer, aided by a 30 over the back nine, finished two strokes ahead of 20-year old amateur Jack Nicklaus.

QUIZ: Who are the only two brothers enshrined in the Baseball Hall of Fame?

Trivia Timeout
Former NFL quarterback Roger Staubach is color-blind.

QUIZ ANSWER: Paul and Lloyd Waner

JUNE 19th

TODAY'S THOUGHT: "I took the two most expensive aspirins in history." —*Wally Pipp, the Yankee first baseman who was replaced by Lou Gehrig, on the headache that kept him on the bench that day*

HISTORY: On this date in 1973 hockey great Gordie Howe came out of retirement, signing with the Houston Aeros of the World Hockey Association.

QUIZ: At the 1968 Masters, I finished tied for first with Bob Goalby. But after signing an incorrect scorecard, I had to settle for second. Who am I?

Trivia Timeout
Two of Howe's teammates on the Aeros were his sons, Mark and Marty.

QUIZ ANSWER: Roberto de Vicenzo

JUNE 20th

TODAY'S THOUGHT: "Boxing: This is the only sport in the world where two guys get paid for doing something they'd be arrested for if they got drunk and did it for nothing." —*Carl Foreman*

HISTORY: On this date in 1960 Floyd Patterson KO'd Ingemar Johansson to regain his heavyweight title, the first boxer in history to do so. Johansson had taken the crown from Patterson a year earlier.

QUIZ: Excluding the British Isles, what country had the first golf course?

Trivia Timeout
The game of darts originated as a training exercise for archers.

QUIZ ANSWER: India, in 1829 — The Royal Calcutta Golf Club

JUNE 21st

TODAY'S THOUGHT: "He's got to raise the level of his talent to the level of his paycheck."
—Charles Barkley, on Nets forward Derrick Coleman

HISTORY: On this date in 1964 Jim Bunning, a father of 10, celebrated Father's Day by throwing a perfect game against the Mets.

QUIZ: This wide receiver gained over 100 yards receiving in Super Bowl I, after a regular season in which he gained fewer than 100 yards. Who was it?

Trivia Timeout

Bunning and Nolan Ryan are the only pitchers to have thrown no-hitters in both the American and National Leagues.

QUIZ ANSWER: Max McGee of the Packers

JUNE 22nd

TODAY'S THOUGHT: "The whole art of pitching is in the wrist." *—Carl Hubbell*

HISTORY: On this date in 1937 Joe Louis began boxing's longest reign as heavyweight champ. The "Brown Bomber" took the crown from James J. Braddock and kept it for over 11 years.

QUIZ: The pitcher who started the first game ever for the Florida Marlins is also the only hurler in Major League baseball history with at least 375 starts and 375 relief appearances. Who is he?

Trivia Timeout

Former New York Jets executive Sonny Werblin was once an agent for actor Ronald Reagan.

QUIZ ANSWER: Charlie Hough

JUNE 23rd

TODAY'S THOUGHT: "A player's got to be kept hungry to become a big leaguer. That's why no boy from a rich family ever made it to the big leagues." —*Joe DiMaggio*

HISTORY: On this date in 1971 Philadelphia's Rick Wise became the answer to a trivia question, becoming the only pitcher to hit two home runs while recording a no-hitter.

QUIZ: After Red Auerbach stepped down, who were the next four Boston coaches?

Trivia Timeout
Danny Biasone "invented" basketball's 24-second shot clock in 1954.

QUIZ ANSWER: Bill Russell, Tom Heinsohn, Tom Sanders and Dave Cowens— all former Celtics players

JUNE 24th

TODAY'S THOUGHT: "Some night you'll catch a punch between the eyes and...see three guys in the ring against you. Pick out the one in the middle and hit him, because he's the one who hit you." —*Jack Dempsey*

HISTORY: On this date in 1922 the American Professional Football Association changed its name to the National Football League.

QUIZ: There are five Major Leaguers with more than 3,000 career hits who have never won a batting title. Four of them are Eddie Collins, Lou Brock, Robin Yount and Dave Winfield. Who's the fifth? (Hint: He achieved this in 2000.)

Trivia Timeout
Curley Lambeau bought the rights to the Packers for $50.

QUIZ ANSWER: Cal Ripken Jr.

JUNE 25th

TODAY'S THOUGHT: "Golf: A game in which a ball one and a half inches in diameter is placed on a ball 8,000 miles in diameter. The object is to hit the small ball but not the larger." —*John Cunningham*

HISTORY: On this date in 1978 Argentina's soccer team upended the Netherlands, 3-1, to win its first World Cup.

QUIZ: Who is the only player to rush for more than 5,000 yards for each of two NFL teams?

Trivia Timeout

The only female athlete not required to undergo a sex test at the 1976 Summer Olympics was Princess Anne of England, who competed in the equestrian events.

QUIZ ANSWER: Eric Dickerson, for the Rams and Colts

JUNE 26th

TODAY'S THOUGHT: "Sweat plus sacrifice equals success." —*Charlie Finley*

HISTORY: On this date in 1916 the Cleveland Indians became the first baseball players with numbers on their uniforms. The Tribe wore the numerals on their sleeves.

QUIZ: Can you name the only player to hit home runs in his first two World Series at bats?

Trivia Timeout

The 1929 Yankees were the first team to wear numbers on the back of their uniforms. Each player's number corresponded with his spot in the batting order.

QUIZ ANSWER: Gene Tenace of the Oakland A's, versus the Reds in the first game of the 1972 Series

JUNE 27th

TODAY'S THOUGHT: "I don't have any handicap. I am all handicap." —*Lyndon Johnson, on golf*

HISTORY: On this date in 1988 Mike Tyson made short work of Michael Spinks to retain his heavyweight title. How short? The champ knocked out Spinks in ninety-one seconds.

QUIZ: Name the first college basketball player to win the Sullivan Award as the nation's top amateur athlete.

Trivia Timeout

Tyson's earnings for the fight amounted to $240,000 per second of work.

QUIZ ANSWER: Bill Bradley of Princeton won the award in 1965.

JUNE 28th

TODAY'S THOUGHT: "If you can't outplay them, outwork them." —*Ben Hogan*

HISTORY: On this date in 1987 Don Baylor received a birthday gift he probably could have done without. Baylor was hit by a pitch for the 244th time, breaking the career record set by Ron Hunt.

QUIZ: What is the name of the trophy that the winning team in the Super Bowl receives?

Trivia Timeout

Johnny Berardino of the St. Louis Browns had his nose insured for a million dollars. It seems that the second baseman was concerned about his other career as an actor on a TV soap opera.

QUIZ ANSWER: The Vince Lombardi Trophy

JUNE 29th

TODAY'S THOUGHT: "The difference between hitting .300 and .270 is a hit and a half a week."
—*Mark Grace, Cubs first baseman*

HISTORY: On this date in 1957 Jackie Fung mistakenly put down the wrong score for one hole and, as a result, was disqualified from the U.S. Open. Had Fung not erred, she would have been in a play-off with Betsy Rawls, who was declared the winner.

QUIZ: In bowling, what number pin is the kingpin?

Trivia Timeout

Boston Braves hurler Charlie "Red" Barrett needed just 58 pitches in a 2-0 shutout of the Cincinnati Reds in 1944.

QUIZ ANSWER: 5

JUNE 30th

TODAY'S THOUGHT: "I'd give up golf if I didn't have so many sweaters." —*Bob Hope*

HISTORY: On this date in 1984 the Los Angeles Express and the Michigan Panthers of the USFL played the longest game in pro football history. The teams went into a third overtime before the Express won, 27-21.

QUIZ: Over which eye does the Los Angeles Raiders' warrior shown on the helmet wear a patch?

Trivia Timeout

Babe Ruth and Lou Gehrig were once fanned in an exhibition game by a teenager — a 17-year old girl named Jackie Mitchell.

QUIZ ANSWER: The right eye

JULY 1st

TODAY'S THOUGHT: "One loss is good for the soul. Too many losses are not good for the coach."
—Knute Rockne

HISTORY: On this date in 1910 Chicago's Comiskey Park opened its gates for the first time.

QUIZ: Three U.S. cities have had teams win both the Super Bowl and the Stanley Cup. Can you identify them?

Trivia Timeout
Runner Carl Lewis never played football or basketball in college but he was drafted by the Dallas Cowboys and the Chicago Bulls in 1984.

QUIZ ANSWER: Pittsburgh (the Steelers and Penguins); Chicago (the Bears and Blackhawks); and New York (the Jets, Giants, Islanders and Rangers)

JULY 2nd

TODAY'S THOUGHT: "You've got to win in sports — that's talent — but you've also got to learn how to remind everybody how you did win, and how often. That comes with experience." *—Billie Jean King*

HISTORY: On this date in 1938 Helen Wills Moody defeated Helen Hull Jacobs to win the Wimbledon championship for the eighth time.

QUIZ: Who is the only college basketball coach to reach the NCAA Final Four in four different decades?

Trivia Timeout
Volleyball, invented by William G. Morgan, was first played in 1895 at the Holyoke, Massachusetts YMCA.

QUIZ ANSWER: Dean Smith of North Carolina, in the '60's, '70's, '80's and '90's

JULY 3rd

TODAY'S THOUGHT: "The game is my wife. It demands loyalty and responsibility, and it gives me back fulfillment and peace." —*Michael Jordan*

HISTORY: On this date in 1983 sprinter Calvin Smith broke the record for the men's 100-meter dash. The same day, at the same track meet, Evelyn Ashford snapped the women's 100-meter mark.

QUIZ: In 1947 this baseball Hall of Famer became the only player to hit 50 or more home runs in a season in which he struck out fewer than 50 times. Who was it?

Trivia Timeout

Ernie Davis became the first black player to be awarded the Heisman Trophy in 1961.

QUIZ ANSWER: Johnny Mize, 51 and 42 respectively

JULY 4th

TODAY'S THOUGHT: "Whoever wants to know the heart and mind of America had better learn baseball." —*Jacques Barzun, philosophy professor*

HISTORY: On this date in 1939 Lou Gehrig bid farewell to his teammates and fans with an emotional speech in which he called himself "the luckiest man on the face of the earth".

QUIZ: Who holds the record for home runs hit in Yankee Stadium?

Trivia Timeout

Gehrig and Babe Ruth feuded for six years — not speaking to each other. The silence was broken when the two embraced and spoke at the Yankee Stadium ceremony.

QUIZ ANSWER: Mickey Mantle, with 266

JULY 5th

TODAY'S THOUGHT: "Drive for show. But putt for dough." —*Bobby Locke*

HISTORY: On this date in 1975 Arthur Ashe became the first black to win the men's singles title at Wimbledon when he defeated Jimmy Connors in four sets. Twenty-eight years earlier to the day, Larry Doby broke the color barrier in the American League, appearing as a pinch-hitter for the Cleveland Indians.

QUIZ: Who coached the 1992 U.S. men's Olympic basketball team?

Trivia Timeout

The odds of converting a 7-10 split in bowling are 2,000,000:1.

QUIZ ANSWER: Chuck Daly

JULY 6th

TODAY'S THOUGHT: "Be quick but never hurry." —*John Wooden*

HISTORY: On this date in 1933 players from the National League and the American League squared off at Comiskey Park for baseball's first All-Star Game.

QUIZ: Who hit the first grand slam in All-Star game history?

Trivia Timeout

The first All-Star Game was planned as part of the festivities for the Chicago World's Fair. Proceeds from the game went to charity.

QUIZ ANSWER: Fred Lynn of the Boston Red Sox, who hit it exactly 50 years after the inaugural All-Star contest, on the same day and in the same park

JULY 7th

TODAY'S THOUGHT: "It got so that I could nip the frosting off a cake with my fastball." —*Satchel Paige*

HISTORY: On this date in 1985 17-year old Boris Becker became the youngest player to win at Wimbledon, beating Kevin Curren in four sets.

QUIZ: When Ralph Sampson played for the Houston Rockets, he was considered half of the team's "Twin Towers". Who was the other "tower"?

Trivia Timeout

Satchel Paige earned his nickname from his job as a redcap at a train station where he carried people's "satchels".

QUIZ ANSWER: Center Hakeem Olajuwon who, with fellow seven-footer Sampson, dominated the Houston skyline

JULY 8th

TODAY'S THOUGHT: "Years ago we discovered the exact point, the dead center of middle age. It occurs when you are too young to take up golf and too old to rush up to the net." —*Franklin P. Adams*

HISTORY: On this date in 1889 John L. Sullivan knocked out Jake Kilrain in the 75th round to win the heavyweight championship. The fight was the last of the bare-knuckle bouts.

QUIZ: Mickey Mantle has hit the most home runs in the World Series, 18. Who is second?

Trivia Timeout

During the bare-knuckle era, rounds were not timed. A round ended when a fighter was knocked down.

QUIZ ANSWER: Babe Ruth, with 15

JULY 9th

TODAY'S THOUGHT: "Games played with the ball, and others of that nature, are too violent for the body and stamp no character on the mind." —*Thomas Jefferson*

HISTORY: On this date in 1984 the Olympic basketball team, led by Michael Jordan and Patrick Ewing, embarrassed the NBA "all-stars", 97-82.

QUIZ: In 1967 the NHL expanded from six teams to twelve. Can you name the newcomers?

Trivia Timeout
A ticket to Super Bowl I cost $10.

QUIZ ANSWER: The expansion clubs were the California Seals, the Los Angeles Kings, the Minnesota North Stars, the Philadelphia Flyers, the Pittsburgh Penguins and the St. Louis Blues.

JULY 10th

TODAY'S THOUGHT: "A winner never whines."
—*Paul Brown*

HISTORY: On this date in 1934 Carl Hubbell fanned Babe Ruth, Lou Gehrig, Jimmie Foxx, Al Simmons and Joe Cronin consecutively in the second All-Star Game.

QUIZ: Besides Carl Hubbell, what other pitcher has fanned five consecutive batters in an All-Star Game?

Trivia Timeout
Andre Dawson once paid a fine for a tantrum he threw after being called out on strikes by writing a check with the notation, "Donation for the blind".

QUIZ ANSWER: Fernando Valenzuela fanned Don Mattingly, Cal Ripken, Jr., Jesse Barfield, Lou Whitaker and Ted Higuera in 1986.

JULY 11th

TODAY'S THOUGHT: "Ryan is the only guy who puts fear in me. Not because he can get you out but because he can kill you."
—*Reggie Jackson, on Nolan Ryan*

HISTORY: On this date in 1985 the Astros' Nolan Ryan became the first man to strike out 4,000 batters.

QUIZ: Name the only two players to win baseball's Triple Crown twice.

Trivia Timeout
Cesar Geronimo was the 3,000th strikeout victim of both Nolan Ryan and Bob Gibson.

QUIZ ANSWER: Rogers Hornsby won the award in 1922 and 1925. Ted Williams did it in 1942 and 1947.

JULY 12th

TODAY'S THOUGHT: "Golf and sex are the only two things you can enjoy without being good at."
—*Jimmy Demaret*

HISTORY: On this date in 1964 Mickey Wright won a play-off over Ruth Jessen to capture her fourth U.S. Women's Open golf tournament. Wright joined Betsy Rawls as the only four-time winners of the Open.

QUIZ: True or false? Tom Seaver only won the Cy Young Award once in his career.

Trivia Timeout
The grand champion in sumo wrestling is called the Yokozuna.

QUIZ ANSWER: False. "Tom Terrific" won the award in 1969, '73 and '75.

JULY 13th

TODAY'S THOUGHT: "In golf you're always breaking a barrier. When you bust it, you set yourself a little higher barrier, and try to break that one."
—*Jack Nicklaus*

HISTORY: On this date in 1963 Cleveland pitcher Early Wynn joined the 300-victory club when he pitched the Indians to a 7-4 win over the Kansas City A's.

QUIZ: Who succeeded the legendary Adolph Rupp as head basketball coach at Kentucky?

Trivia Timeout
The baseball phrase "around the horn" comes from the nautical term for a ship sailing between the Atlantic and the Pacific before the Panama Canal was completed.

QUIZ ANSWER: Joe B. Hall

JULY 14th

TODAY'S THOUGHT: "You never get ahead of anyone as long as you try to get even with him." —*Lou Holtz*

HISTORY: On this date in 1951 Citation, the 1948 Triple Crown winner, captured the Hollywood Cup and became the first thoroughbred to top a million dollars in career winnings. That same day at Monmouth Park in New Jersey, CBS televised the Molly Pitcher Handicap in color, a sports first.

QUIZ: Who was the last NFL scoring leader to do double-duty as a kicker and a running back — allowing him to score both a touchdown and the point after?

Trivia Timeout
Fighter Rocky Graziano was born "Rocco Barbella".

QUIZ ANSWER: Paul Hornung of the Green Bay Packers

JULY 15th

TODAY'S THOUGHT: "Competitive golf is played mainly on a five-and-a-half-inch course — the space between your ears." *—Bobby Jones*

HISTORY: On this date in 1923 Bobby Jones edged Bobby Cruikshank by two strokes in an 18-hole playoff to win the U.S. Open. It was the first major title for the 21-year old amateur.

QUIZ: Who is the only man inducted into the Baseball Hall of Fame and the Pro Football Hall of Fame?

Trivia Timeout
The Dallas Cowboys were the first NFL team to display numbers on the sides of their pants.

QUIZ ANSWER: Cal Hubbard, who played for the Green Bay Packers and umpired in the American League

JULY 16th

TODAY'S THOUGHT: "There are no pleasures in a fight but some of my fights have been a pleasure to win." *—Muhammad Ali*

HISTORY: On this date in 1947 Rocky Graziano dethroned Tony Zale as World Middleweight Champion. Graziano knocked out Zale in the sixth round.

QUIZ: Who was the last National League player to bat .400 for a season?

Trivia Timeout
Bowling pins are made of maple.

QUIZ ANSWER: New York Giants first baseman Bill Terry hit .401 in 1930.

JULY 17th

TODAY'S THOUGHT: "Win this one for the 'Gipper'."
—*Knute Rockne*

HISTORY: On this date in 1941 the longest hitting streak in Major League baseball history came to an end. Cleveland held Joe DiMaggio hitless in three at bats to stop the Yankee Clipper's streak.

QUIZ: Exactly who was the "Gipper"?

> ### Trivia Timeout
> *After being stopped at 56, DiMaggio went on to hit in 16 more games in a row.*

QUIZ ANSWER: The "Gipper" — whose untimely death from pneumonia provided the Notre Dame football team with an emotional lift — was George Gipp, an All-American halfback for the Fighting Irish.

JULY 18th

TODAY'S THOUGHT: "You may glory in a team triumphant, but fall in love with a team in defeat."
—*Roger Kahn*

HISTORY: On this date in 1976 14-year old Nadia Comaneci of Romania recorded the first perfect score in Olympic gymnastics.

QUIZ: Of all the players selected as the number one pick in the NBA draft in the 70's, only one won the Rookie of the Year award. Who was it?

> ### Trivia Timeout
> *The minimum diameter allowed for a golf ball is 1.68 inches.*

QUIZ ANSWER: Kareem Abdul-Jabbar of the Milwaukee Bucks was honored as the NBA's best rookie in 1970.

JULY 19th

TODAY'S THOUGHT: "Lawn tennis is boring. It will never catch on."
—*Spense Gore, first Wimbledon champion*

HISTORY: On this date in 1877 about two hundred people turned out to watch the first Wimbledon tennis championship.

QUIZ: Name the only Major League pitcher with 300 wins to record all his victories with one team.

Trivia Timeout
The Wimbledon Club originally was formed to play croquet.

QUIZ ANSWER: Walter Johnson notched all of his 416 victories with the Washington Senators. Christy Mathewson came close — winning 372 for the Giants and one for the Reds.

JULY 20th

TODAY'S THOUGHT: "Never argue with people who buy ink by the gallon." —*Tommy Lasorda, on the Press*

HISTORY: On this date in 1973 the Chicago White Sox' Wilbur Wood became the last hurler to start both halves of a doubleheader—losing both games.

QUIZ: Four golfers have had 10 or more wins on the PGA Tour before reaching their 30th birthdays. Jack Nicklaus had 30 and Arnold Palmer had 10. Who are the other two?

Trivia Timeout
St. Louis Cardinals pitcher Hi Bell was the last man to start and win both games of a twin-bill, on July 19, 1924.

QUIZ ANSWER: Johnny Miller notched 17 wins and Tom Watson had 16 before turning 30 years old.

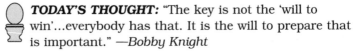

JULY 21st

TODAY'S THOUGHT: "The key is not the 'will to win'...everybody has that. It is the will to prepare that is important." —*Bobby Knight*

HISTORY: On this date in 1979 Seve Ballesteros won his first British Open at Royal Lythan, England.

QUIZ: Despite winning nine NBA championships, this man was named Coach of the Year only once. Can you name him?

Trivia Timeout

In Bob Feller's Major League debut, the future Hall of Famer struck out the first eight batters that he faced.

QUIZ ANSWER: Red Auerbach of the Boston Celtics was so honored in 1965. Ironically, the award is now called the Arnold "Red" Auerbach Trophy.

JULY 22nd

TODAY'S THOUGHT: "He went from Cy Young to sayonora in a year." —*Graig Nettles, on Sparky Lyle*

HISTORY: On this date in 1952 American Bob Richards won the gold medal in the pole vault at the Summer Olympics in Helsinki.

QUIZ: Two big leaguers have hit 50 or more home runs in a season for two different teams. Name them.

Trivia Timeout

Bob Richards was a theology professor and was dubbed "The Vaulting Vicar".

QUIZ ANSWER: Jimmie Foxx (for the Philadelphia A's and the Boston Red Sox) and Mark McGwire (for the Oakland A's and the St. Louis Cardinals)

JULY 23rd

TODAY'S THOUGHT: "You win some, you lose some and some get rained out, but you gotta suit up for them all." —*J. Askenberg*

HISTORY: On this date in 1989 Greg LeMond won cycling's Tour de France for the second time. LeMond trailed going into the final day of the race, but rallied to win by eight seconds, the smallest winning margin ever.

QUIZ: Between 1959 and 1962 the Major Leagues played two All-Star Games a year. This pitcher was the only hurler to start both of the games in the same season. Who was it?

Trivia Timeout
Pee Wee Reese's real first name is Harold.

QUIZ ANSWER: Dodger Don Drysdale, in 1959

JULY 24th

TODAY'S THOUGHT: "Hitting is better than sex." —*Reggie Jackson*

HISTORY: On this date in 1983 George Brett's home run against the Yankees was disallowed when the umpires ruled that the pine tar on his bat went too far up the handle. The decision was later overturned by the League.

QUIZ: Which NFL team was the first to play its home games in a domed stadium?

Trivia Timeout
Sportswriter Caswell Adams coined the name "Ivy League".

QUIZ ANSWER: The Houston Oilers began playing in the Astrodome in 1968.

JULY 25th

TODAY'S THOUGHT: "Golf is an awkward set of bodily contortions designed to produce a graceful result."
—Tommy Armour

HISTORY: On this date in 1976 Edwin Moses won the gold medal for the 400-meter hurdles at the Summer Olympics in Montreal.

QUIZ: Name the college that holds the record for the most consecutive winning seasons in basketball.

A: UCLA B: Louisville C: North Carolina D: Indiana

Trivia Timeout
Mario Andretti, John Elway and Jose Canseco are all twins.

QUIZ ANSWER: B — From 1944-45 until 1989-90 Louisville strung together 46 straight winning seasons. In 1990-91 the Cardinals slipped to 14-16.

JULY 26th

TODAY'S THOUGHT: "When you come to the fork in the road, take it."
—Yogi Berra, master of malaprops, giving directions

HISTORY: On this date in 1952 Bob Mathias of the U.S. won the gold medal in the decathlon at the Summer Olympics in Helsinki, becoming the first person to win two straight gold medals in the history of the event.

QUIZ: If all the Major League baseball players — past and present — were lined up alphabetically, who would be first?

Trivia Timeout
Bob Lilly, a defensive lineman from Texas Christian University, was the first draft pick in Dallas Cowboys history.

QUIZ ANSWER: Henry Aaron

JULY 27th

TODAY'S THOUGHT: "These are the saddest of possible words — Tinker to Evers to Chance. Trio of Bear Cubs and fleeter than birds — Tinker to Evers to Chance." —*Franklin Adams, writer, on the Cubs Hall of Fame infield*

HISTORY: On this date in 1985 Steve Cram knocked more than a full second off the record for the mile run. His winning time of 3:46.32 was the tops in a race in which eight runners finished under 3:50.

QUIZ: Name the hockey movie starring Paul Newman.

Trivia Timeout

Former NBA guard Kiki Vandeweghe's mother was a Miss America.

QUIZ ANSWER: "Slapshot"

JULY 28th

TODAY'S THOUGHT: "We Americans are a peculiar people. We are for the underdog no matter how much of a dog he is."
—*"Happy" Chandler, onetime baseball commissioner*

HISTORY: On this date in 1991 Dennis Martinez became the first Latin American pitcher to hurl a perfect game in the Majors as the Expos beat the Dodgers, 2-0.

QUIZ: Who was the first coach of the NBA's Phoenix Suns?

Trivia Timeout

Ron Hassey was the catcher for Montreal that day. He was also behind the plate for Cleveland when the Indians' Len Barker threw a perfect game against Toronto in 1981.

QUIZ ANSWER: Johnny Kerr

JULY 29th

TODAY'S THOUGHT: "The harder you work, the luckier you get." —*Gary Player*

HISTORY: On this date in 1983 Steve Garvey's bid to top Lou Gehrig's consecutive-game streak ended at 1,207 games when he dislocated his thumb in a collision at home plate.

QUIZ: Can you name the only member of a losing team to be selected MVP in a Super Bowl?

Trivia Timeout
Dan Driessen of the Reds was the National League's first designated hitter, DHing in the 1976 World Series.

QUIZ ANSWER: Chuck Howley of Dallas, who intercepted two passes in Super Bowl V against the Colts — The Cowboys lost, 16-13.

JULY 30th

TODAY'S THOUGHT: "Sports is the only entertainment where, no matter how many times you go back, you'll never know the ending." —*Neil Simon*

HISTORY: On this date in 1968 Washington Senators shortstop Ron Hansen turned in the first unassisted triple play in the Major Leagues in more than 41 years. Hansen didn't fare as well at the plate, however, fanning four times against the Indians.

QUIZ: Only once in NFL history has a player rushed for 99 yards on one play. Who did it?

Trivia Timeout
Miniature golf was originally called "Tom Thumb Golf".

QUIZ ANSWER: Tony Dorsett of the Dallas Cowboys, who went the distance in a 1983 game against Minnesota

JULY 31st

TODAY'S THOUGHT: "All fighters are prostitutes and all promoters are pimps." —*Larry Holmes*

HISTORY: On this date in 1976 Sugar Ray Leonard became the fifth U.S. boxer to win a gold medal at the Montreal Summer Olympics.

QUIZ: Pete Maravich finished his NBA career with the Boston Celtics. Do you know what team made him their number one draft choice in 1970?

Trivia Timeout

Also winning the gold that year were Leon and Michael Spinks, Howard Davis and Leo Randolph.

QUIZ ANSWER: Pistol Pete was the top choice of the Atlanta Hawks.

AUGUST 1st

TODAY'S THOUGHT: "Golf is a non-violent game played violently from within." —*Bob Toski*

HISTORY: On this date in 1972 San Diego first baseman Nate Colbert lit up the scoreboard in a doubleheader against Atlanta. Colbert hit five homers and drove in 13 runs as the Padres swept the Braves.

QUIZ: What stadium was used for a World Series, a Super Bowl and an NCAA Basketball Final?

Trivia Timeout

Colbert's five home runs tied a record set 18 years before by Stan Musial. In attendance at that Cardinals-Giants game in 1954 was an eight-year old fan...Nate Colbert.

QUIZ ANSWER: Minnesota's Hubert H. Humphrey Metrodome

AUGUST 2nd

TODAY'S THOUGHT: "Never let your head hang down. Never give up and sit down and grieve. Find another way. And don't pray when it rains if you don't pray when the sun shines." —*Satchel Paige*

HISTORY: On this date in 1984 super heavyweight Jeff Blatnick won the Olympic gold medal for Greco-Roman wrestling capping his two-year battle against cancer.

QUIZ: The 1940 NFL Championship Game is remembered for the most one-sided score in pro football history. Who were the teams and what was the score?

Trivia Timeout

The Tour de France is 2,025 miles long.

QUIZ ANSWER: The Chicago Bears blanked the Washington Redskins, 73-0.

AUGUST 3rd

TODAY'S THOUGHT: "You can't be too rich, too thin, or have too many Penn State linebackers."
—*Marv Levy, Buffalo Bills coach*

HISTORY: On this date in 1986 the NFL redefined the word "football" in England, playing the first game ever on British soil, an exhibition game between the Chicago Bears and the Dallas Cowboys.

QUIZ: On this day in 1960 the Tigers and Indians traded managers. Can you name them?

Trivia Timeout
In the United Kingdom, an exhibition match in soccer — as it would be called in the U.S. — translates as a "friendly" match.

QUIZ ANSWER: Jimmy Dykes went to Cleveland; Joe Gordon moved to the Tigers.

AUGUST 4th

TODAY'S THOUGHT: "The more violent the body contact of the sports you watch, the lower your class."
—*Paul Fussell*

HISTORY: On this date in 1982 Joel Youngblood, traded from the Mets to the Expos, became the first Major Leaguer to get a hit for two different teams in two different cities on the same day.

QUIZ: Who is the only player to rush for 1,000 yards in a season in both the AFL and NFL?

Trivia Timeout
Goodyear names its blimps for the winners of the America's Cup.

QUIZ ANSWER: Mike Garrett, with the 1967 Kansas City Chiefs (AFL) and 1972 San Diego Chargers (NFL)

AUGUST 5th

TODAY'S THOUGHT: "Baseball is the most intellectual game because most of the action goes on in your head." —*Henry Kissinger*

HISTORY: On this date in 1936 Jesse Owens edged out Mack Robinson to win the 200-meter dash at the Summer Olympics in Berlin. It was Owen's third of four gold medals — an embarrassment to host, Aryan-supremacist Adolph Hitler.

QUIZ: True or false? Celtics great Bill Russell never scored 50 points in an NBA game.

Trivia Timeout

Few people remember Olympian Mack Robinson but many recall his younger brother, baseball pioneer Jackie Robinson.

QUIZ ANSWER: True

AUGUST 6th

TODAY'S THOUGHT: "When you win, nothing hurts." —*Joe Namath*

HISTORY: On this date in 1926 Gertrude Ederle became the first American woman to swim the English Channel.

QUIZ: What baseball Hall of Famer was the last manager of the Washington Senators?

Trivia Timeout

Ederle trained for her Channel crossing by swimming in New York harbor.

QUIZ ANSWER: Ted Williams managed the Senators from 1969 to 1971. He then moved with the club to Texas, piloting the Rangers in 1972.

AUGUST 7th

TODAY'S THOUGHT: "Of all major team sports, baseball alone acknowledges perfect games in its record book." —*Good Reading Magazine*

HISTORY: On this date in 1992 16-year old tennis phenom Jennifer Capriati won the Olympic Gold Medal with a victory over Steffi Graf.

QUIZ: Who was the first NHL player to score more than 100 points (goals and assists) in a season?

Trivia Timeout

Mickey Mantle's original uniform number with the Yankees was 6 — not 7.

QUIZ ANSWER: Phil Esposito of the Boston Bruins scored 126 points in the 1968-69 season.

AUGUST 8th

TODAY'S THOUGHT: "Putting lights on Wrigley Field is like putting aluminum siding on the Sistine Chapel." —*Roger Simon, columnist*

HISTORY: On this date in 1988 the lights came on in Chicago as the Phillies and the Cubs met in the first ever night game at Wrigley Field.

QUIZ: In soccer's World Cup, the teams of two nations are guaranteed entry into the tournament. Which two?

Trivia Timeout

Aquatic actress Esther Williams was a champion swimmer and a member of the 1940 U.S. Olympic squad. (The team never made it to Helsinki due to WWII forcing the cancellation of the Games.)

QUIZ ANSWER: The host and defending champion

AUGUST 9th

TODAY'S THOUGHT: "Catching a fly ball is a pleasure, but knowing what to do with it is a business."
—*Tommy Henrich*

HISTORY: On this date in 1988 the Edmonton Oilers shocked the NHL by trading superstar Wayne Gretzky to the Los Angeles Kings.

QUIZ: This player-manager with the Indians pencilled himself into the lineup on Opening Day in 1975 and then justified his decision with a home run in his first at bat. Can you name him?

Trivia Timeout
Pitching great Sandy Koufax was born Sanford Braun.

QUIZ ANSWER: Frank Robinson, who also made his debut that day as the first black manager

AUGUST 10th

TODAY'S THOUGHT: "Hurting people is my business."
—*Sugar Ray Robinson*

HISTORY: On this date in 1971 Minnesota Twin Harmon Killebrew became the tenth player in Major League history to hit 500 home runs when he teed off against Orioles pitcher Mike Cuellar.

QUIZ: Do you know the five events that comprise the modern pentathlon?

Trivia Timeout
Australian Niles Lied once drove a golf ball one and one-half miles — across an ice cap at Mawson Base, Antarctica.

QUIZ ANSWER: Riding, fencing, shooting, swimming and running are the five events.

AUGUST 11th

TODAY'S THOUGHT: "Knute Rockne liked 'bad losers'. He said 'good losers' lose too often." —*George Allen*

HISTORY: On this date in 1991 25-year old John Daly stunned the golf world by winning the PGA Championship. Daly became the first rookie in 15 years to win a major and the first in 47 years to win the PGA on his first try.

QUIZ: For what team did Hall of Famer Warren Spahn hurl his last game?

Trivia Timeout

Daly got into the tournament when six golfers dropped out, including Nick Price. Price's caddy accompanied Daly in his winning effort.

QUIZ ANSWER: The San Francisco Giants

AUGUST 12th

TODAY'S THOUGHT: "Say this for big league baseball — it is beyond any question the greatest conversation piece ever invented." —*Bruce Catton*

HISTORY: On this date in 1936 American diver Marjorie Gestring won the Olympic gold medal in the springboard event. Gestring was 13 years old — the youngest gold medal winner ever.

QUIZ: What team won the first AFL championship?

Trivia Timeout

At age 19 rocker Rod Stewart abandoned a pro soccer career in Scotland to pursue his musical career.

QUIZ ANSWER: The Houston Oilers beat the Los Angeles Chargers, 24-16, in the inaugural AFL championship game in 1960.

AUGUST 13th

TODAY'S THOUGHT: "Selecting a stroke is like selecting a wife. To each his own." —*Ben Hogan*

HISTORY: On this date in 1969 acting commissioner of Major League baseball Bowie Kuhn was formally appointed to the position. Kuhn's "temporary" assignment lasted until 1984.

QUIZ: In 1991 this college basketball player broke Pete Maravich's Division I single-game scoring record when he tallied 72 points against Loyola Marymount. Who was it?

Trivia Timeout

All race horses celebrate their birthdays on January 1, regardless of when they were born.

QUIZ ANSWER: Kevin Bradshaw of U.S. International University

AUGUST 14th

TODAY'S THOUGHT: "A complete ballplayer today is one who can hit, field, run, throw and pick the right agent." —*Robert Lurie, owner of the San Francisco Giants*

HISTORY: On this date in 1987 Oakland rookie outfielder Mark McGwire hit his 39th homer of the year. That set a new record for home runs in a season by a rookie, a mark that McGwire would extend to 49.

QUIZ: When this shortstop won the NL Gold Glove in 1993 he broke a string of 13 consecutive Gold Gloves for another National League shortstop. Name both.

Trivia Timeout

Baseball's Indians were originally called the Spiders.

QUIZ ANSWER: Jay Bell of the Pirates beat out perennial winner Ozzie Smith of the Cardinals.

AUGUST 15th

TODAY'S THOUGHT: "When you win, nothing hurts."
—Joe Namath

HISTORY: On this date in 1950 Ezzard Charles defended his heavyweight title for the third time since he succeeded Joe Louis as champ.

QUIZ: Can you name the only golfer to win the U.S. Open, British Open and the Masters in the same year?

Trivia Timeout

Charles originally won the title, decisioning Jersey Joe Walcott, in an elimination bout after Joe Louis retired.

QUIZ ANSWER: Ben Hogan, in 1953 — He was denied a chance to win the Grand Slam because the fourth event, the PGA Championship, conflicted with the British Open.

AUGUST 16th

TODAY'S THOUGHT: "Every obnoxious fan has a wife home who dominates him." *—Al McGuire*

HISTORY: On this date in 1954 "Sports Illustrated" made its debut. An action shot of Milwaukee Braves third baseman Ed Mathews was on the first cover.

QUIZ: Roger Bannister was the first miler to break the four minute barrier. Can you name the first runner to cover a mile in less than 3:50?

Trivia Timeout

Amos Alonzo Stagg coached college football for 71 years — longer than anyone else in the history of the game.

QUIZ ANSWER: John Walker of New Zealand ran the mile in 3:49.4 in 1975.

AUGUST 17th

TODAY'S THOUGHT: "The important thing is to learn a lesson every time you lose." —*John McEnroe*

HISTORY: On this date in 1938 Henry Armstrong decisioned Lou Ambers to win the lightweight boxing championship. Armstrong, who was already wearing the welterweight and featherweight belts, thus became the first boxer to hold titles in three weight classes at the same time.

QUIZ: This baseball team set a record for futility when it lost its first 21 games of the season in 1988. Can you name these low-flying birds?

Trivia Timeout

"Boog" Powell's real first name is John.

QUIZ ANSWER: The Baltimore Orioles

AUGUST 18th

TODAY'S THOUGHT: "I want to be remembered as a ballplayer who gave all he had to give."
—*Roberto Clemente*

HISTORY: On this date in 1992 Boston Celtics forward Larry Bird announced his retirement from the game. Bird, who along with Magic Johnson was credited with reviving the slumbering NBA, was Rookie of the Year in 1980 and a three-time MVP.

QUIZ: Who were the head coaches in Super Bowl I?

Trivia Timeout

Don Chaney is the only Celtic to have been a teammate of both Bill Russell and Larry Bird.

QUIZ ANSWER: Vince Lombardi coached the Packers while Hank Stram patrolled the sidelines for the Chiefs.

AUGUST 19th

TODAY'S THOUGHT: "Golf...a young man's vice and an old man's penance." —*Irvin S. Cobb*

HISTORY: On this date in 1951 three-foot, seven-inch Eddie Gaedel pinch hit for the Browns against the Tigers. Wearing the number "1/8", Gaedel — a brainchild of owner Bill Veeck — walked on four pitches.

QUIZ: From 1964 to 1969 UCLA won five of six NCAA basketball titles. Who was champ the other time?

Trivia Timeout

Veeck's stunt was not without precedent. In the 30's, Red Sox manager Joe Cronin sent his three-foot, six-inch tall mascot to the plate in an exhibition game.

QUIZ ANSWER: Texas Western, now known as Texas-El Paso, won the title in 1966.

AUGUST 20th

TODAY'S THOUGHT: "Excessive golfing dwarfs the intellect. And this is to be wondered at, when we consider that the more fatuously vacant the mind is, the better for play." —*Sir Walter Simpson*

HISTORY: On this date in 1974 Nolan Ryan struck out 19 batters, but lost, 1-0, in 11 innings to Detroit's Mickey Lolich.

QUIZ: Who is the all-time NFL leader in quarterback sacks?

Trivia Timeout

Catcher Carlton Fisk reversed himself when he went from the Red Sox to the White Sox. "Pudge" wore "27" on his uniform in Boston, switching to "72" in Chicago.

QUIZ ANSWER: Reggie White

AUGUST 21st

TODAY'S THOUGHT: "Win any way you can as long as you can get away with it." —*Leo Durocher*

HISTORY: On this date in 1914 golfer Walter Hagen notched his first big win, taking the U.S. Open.

QUIZ: Who was the first player to hit 40 or more home runs and steal 40 or more bases in the same season?

Trivia Timeout

Hector "Toe" Blake is the only hockey player to win the Hart Memorial Trophy and later coach a Stanley Cup winner. Blake skated to the MVP award with the Canadiens in 1939 and later led Montreal to eight NHL titles, a record.

QUIZ ANSWER: Jose Canseco, who in 1988 hit 42 homers and swiped 40 bases for the Oakland A's

AUGUST 22nd

TODAY'S THOUGHT: "Kill the body and the head will die." —*Joe Frazier*

HISTORY: On this date in 1851 the first ever international yacht race took place, in the English Channel off the Isle of Wight. The sole U.S. entry, the *America*, outdistanced 17 other boats in the event that is now known as the America's Cup.

QUIZ: What two new events besides baseball were added to the 1992 Summer Olympics in Barcelona?

Trivia Timeout

Carl Yastrzemski was the last player to get a hit off Satchel Paige. At the age of 59, Paige pitched three innings for the Kansas City A's, yielding only a double to "Yaz".

QUIZ ANSWER: Women's judo and badminton

AUGUST 23rd

TODAY'S THOUGHT: "Sports and religion are what have made America what it is today." —*Woody Hayes*

HISTORY: On this date in 1936 a seventeen-year old pitcher named Bob Feller made a spectacular debut for the Cleveland Indians. The young right-hander struck out 17 while allowing only six hits in a 4-1 victory over the St. Louis Browns.

QUIZ: Who is the only man to play for both the Seattle Pilots and the Seattle Mariners?

Trivia Timeout
Before wooden tees were invented, golfers used sand to "tee" up the ball.

QUIZ ANSWER: Pitcher Diego Segui

AUGUST 24th

TODAY'S THOUGHT: "Almost the only place in life where a sacrifice is really appreciated."
—*Mark Belaire, on baseball*

HISTORY: On this date in 1988 Minnesota North Star Dino Ciccarelli served two hours for hitting Toronto's Luke Richardson in the head with his hockey stick. Ciccarelli earned the dubious distinction of being the first player to spend time in jail for an infraction on the ice.

QUIZ: In 1965 the Chicago Bears had two first-round choices in the NFL draft. Can you name these two Hall-of-Famers?

Trivia Timeout
Lou Gehrig made the first ever All-Star error.

QUIZ ANSWER: Gale Sayers and Dick Butkus

AUGUST 25th

TODAY'S THOUGHT: "Ronald Reagan has held the two most demeaning jobs in the country — president of the United States and radio broadcaster of the Chicago Cubs." —*George Will*

HISTORY: On this date in 1922 the Cubs blew a 25-6 lead but held on to beat the Phillies, 26-23, in the highest-scoring game in Major League history.

QUIZ: True or false? Outfielders Mickey Mantle and Willie Mays both played shortstop in the Majors.

Trivia Timeout
Ted St. Martin made a place for himself in "Guinness" when he sank 2,036 consecutive basketball free throws.

QUIZ ANSWER: True — Mantle played short seven times, while Mays was pencilled in there twice.

AUGUST 26th

TODAY'S THOUGHT: "The ball is round and the floor is smooth." —*Red Auerbach, on basketball's simplicity*

HISTORY: On this date in 1939 a Major League baseball game was televised for the first time. New York station W2XBS broadcast a doubleheader between the Reds and Dodgers at Ebbets Field with Red Barber calling the game.

QUIZ: Three pitchers have had the distinction of hurling a no-hitter, winning a Cy Young Award and being named World Series MVP. Sandy Koufax was one. Who were the other two?

Trivia Timeout
A soccer goal is eight yards wide and eight feet high.

QUIZ ANSWER: Bob Gibson and Bret Saberhagen

AUGUST 27th

TODAY'S THOUGHT: "Beware the big play; the 80-yard drive is better than the 80-yard pass."
—*Fran Tarkenton*

HISTORY: On this date in 1982 Rickey Henderson stole third against Milwaukee for his 119th stolen base of the year, breaking the record set by Lou Brock in 1974. Henderson finished the season with 130 steals.

QUIZ: What's the name of the trophy given to the champion of the Canadian Football League?

Trivia Timeout
Heavyweight boxing champ Jack Dempsey bought a Rolls-Royce after each successful title fight — six in all.

QUIZ ANSWER: The Grey Cup

AUGUST 28th

TODAY'S THOUGHT: "I prefer rugby to soccer. When soccer players start biting off each others' ears again, maybe I'll like it better." —*Elizabeth Taylor*

HISTORY: On this date in 1977 Brazilian soccer legend Pele played his final North American Soccer League game, leading the New York Cosmos to the championship.

QUIZ: True or false? During World War II the depleted rosters of the Philadelphia Eagles and the Pittsburgh Steelers were combined to form a team called the Steagles.

Trivia Timeout
Pele's real name is Edson Arantes do Nascimento.

QUIZ ANSWER: True

AUGUST 29th

TODAY'S THOUGHT: "Football players, like prostitutes, are in the business of ruining their bodies for the pleasure of strangers." —*Merle Kessler*

HISTORY: On this date in 1950 the International Olympic Committee voted to allow West Germany and Japan to compete in the 1952 Games.

QUIZ: Ty Cobb, at .367, has the highest career batting average in Major League history. Who's second?

Trivia Timeout

Entertainer Ricky Nelson, while appearing on "The Adventures of Ozzie and Harriet" and pursuing a singing career, found time to take up tennis, reaching the finals in the Oregon State boys tournament.

QUIZ ANSWER: Rogers Hornsby, who batted .358

AUGUST 30th

TODAY'S THOUGHT: "I learned that you cannot be taught anything by anyone but yourself."
—*Jean-Claude Killy, on ski instruction*

HISTORY: On this date in 1991 Mike Powell broke the longest-standing record in track and field when he topped the mark set by Bob Beamon in the long jump at the 1968 Summer Olympics.

QUIZ: The Pittsburgh Steelers beat whom to become the first team to win four Super Bowls?

Trivia Timeout

Tongue-wagging Michael Jordan acquired this odd habit from his father, who did the same thing when working on his car.

QUIZ ANSWER: The Rams, in Super Bowl XIV

AUGUST 31st

TODAY'S THOUGHT: "I never had a bad night in my life, but I've had a few bad mornings." —*Lefty Gomez*

HISTORY: On this date in 1881 the first U.S. Lawn Tennis Association Championships were held in Newport, Rhode Island. Twenty-five men entered the singles competition, with Richard D. Sears emerging as the winner.

QUIZ: This NBA player was the first to win back-to-back MVP awards. Can you name him?

Trivia Timeout
The U.S. Lawn Tennis Championships are now known as the U.S. Open.

QUIZ ANSWER: Willis Reed of the Knicks in 1972 and '73

SEPTEMBER 1st

TODAY'S THOUGHT: "College football would be more interesting if the faculty played instead of the students — there would be a great increase in broken arms, legs and necks." —*H.L. Mencken*

HISTORY: On this date in 1984 Mississippi Valley State drubbed Kentucky State, 86-0. Quarterback Willie Totten hit 37 of 55 passes for 699 yards and nine touchdowns.

QUIZ: This Yankees manager won the pennant in his first three years at the helm. Who was he?

Trivia Timeout
Totten's favorite receiver that day pulled down 17 passes for 294 yards and five TD's. His name? Jerry Rice.

QUIZ ANSWER: Ralph Houk, in 1961, '62 and '63

SEPTEMBER 2nd

TODAY'S THOUGHT: "I hate to lose more than I like to win." —*Jimmy Connors*

HISTORY: On this date in 1972 Dave Wottle passed three runners in the final stretch of the 800-meters to win the gold at the Summer Olympics in Munich.

QUIZ: Which basketball player has scored the most career points in NCAA Tournament play?

Trivia Timeout
Former Washington Redskins placekicker Mark Moseley wore five pairs of socks on his kicking foot.

QUIZ ANSWER: Christian Laettner of Duke, who tallied 407 points in 23 games

SEPTEMBER 3rd

TODAY'S THOUGHT: "If Howard Cosell was a sport, it would be roller derby." —*Jimmy Cannon*

HISTORY: On this date in 1990 Chicago White Sox reliever Bobby Thigpen earned his 47th save of the season and a place in Major League history. Thigpen, who finished the year with 57 saves, broke Dave Righetti's record of 46 set in 1986.

QUIZ: What player holds the NFL record for scoring the most touchdowns in a season?

Trivia Timeout
Pitcher Joe Niekro hit only one home run in his big league career. It came off his brother, Phil.

QUIZ ANSWER: John Riggins of the Washington Redskins, who scored 24 TD's in 1983

SEPTEMBER 4th

TODAY'S THOUGHT: "The trick is growing up without getting old."—*Casey Stengel*

HISTORY: On this date in 1972 American swimmer Mark Spitz anchored the 4x100-meter relay to win his seventh gold medal of the Summer Games. Before Spitz, no one had won more than five gold medals.

QUIZ: Name the first catcher to hit 30 or more homers in his rookie season in the Majors.

Trivia Timeout
It took 42 years and almost 10,000 games before the Harlem Globetrotters actually played in Harlem. Their first appearance "uptown" was in 1969.

QUIZ ANSWER: Mike Piazza of the Los Angeles Dodgers, who hit 35 round-trippers in 1993

SEPTEMBER 5th

TODAY'S THOUGHT: "Sports begets tumultuous strife and wrath, and wrath begets fierce quarrels and war to the death." —*Horace*

HISTORY: On this date in 1972 Palestinian terrorists broke into the Olympic Village in Munich and took a group of Israeli athletes hostage for the avowed purpose of freeing Arab guerillas held in prisons in Israel. Seven Israeli athletes and five of the terrorists were killed.

QUIZ: Two head coaches in the NFL have won more than 300 games. Who are they?

Trivia Timeout

Idi Amin, the former leader of Uganda, was that country's heavyweight boxing champ from 1951 to 1960.

QUIZ ANSWER: Don Shula and George Halas

SEPTEMBER 6th

TODAY'S THOUGHT: "A second-guesser is one who don't know anything about the first guess, and he's one who needs two guesses to get one right."
—*Tommy Lasorda*

HISTORY: On this date in 1974 Chris Evert's winning streak was snapped at 55 matches when she lost to Evonne Goolagong in the semifinals of the U.S. Open.

QUIZ: Besides Jack Nicklaus, who was the only other golfer to win the Masters twice in the 70's?

Trivia Timeout

In a game in 1963 California Angels pitcher Paul Foytack gave up four consecutive home runs.

QUIZ ANSWER: Gary Player

SEPTEMBER 7th

TODAY'S THOUGHT: "Paul Brown treated his players as if he bought them at auction with a ring in their noses." —*Jim Murray, columnist*

HISTORY: On this date in 1993 Mark Whiten of the St. Louis Cardinals tied three Major League records in a doubleheader against Cincinnati. Whiten had four homers and 12 runs-batted-in in the nightcap of the twin-bill, totaling 13 RBI's for the day.

QUIZ: What NHL goalie was the first to wear a mask?

Trivia Timeout

In the 70's the Macon, Georgia minor league hockey team was called the Macon Whoopies after a song of almost the same name, "Makin' Whoopie".

QUIZ ANSWER: Jacques Plante, of the Montreal Canadiens

SEPTEMBER 8th

TODAY'S THOUGHT: "A businessman is one who talks golf all morning at the office and business all afternoon on the links." —*Anonymous*

HISTORY: On this date in 1965 Bert Campaneris of the A's played an inning at each defensive position, a Major League first.

QUIZ: I was the first player in the AFL or NFL to catch 100 passes in a season. Who am I?

Trivia Timeout

Three years later Cesar Tovar of the Twins became the second man to play all the positions in one game. The first man to face him when he took the mound...Bert Campaneris.

QUIZ ANSWER: Lionel Taylor, of the Denver Broncos

SEPTEMBER 9th

TODAY'S THOUGHT: "Trade a player a year too early rather than a year too late." —*Branch Rickey*

HISTORY: On this date in 1965 Bob Hendley of the Cubs tossed a one-hitter against the Dodgers and lost. Sandy Koufax got the decision on the strength of his fourth career no-hitter and his first perfect game. The Dodger southpaw struck out 14 of the 27 batters he faced.

QUIZ: What National League baseball park was formerly known as Weeghman Park?

Trivia Timeout

Koufax's battery-mate that day was Jeff Torborg, who was also behind the plate for the California Angels eight years later when Nolan Ryan threw his first no-hitter.

QUIZ ANSWER: Wrigley Field

SEPTEMBER 10th

TODAY'S THOUGHT: "If you're stupid enough to whiff, you should be smart enough to forget it."
—*Arnold Palmer*

HISTORY: On this date in 1974 Lou Brock tied Maury Wills' season stolen base mark in the first inning, then broke it in the seventh with his 105th steal of the year. Brock ended the season with 118 stolen bases.

QUIZ: Who's the only NHL team to come back from a three-games-to-none deficit in the Stanley Cup finals?

Trivia Timeout

Of all the players eligible, Roger Maris remains the only two-time MVP not elected to the Baseball Hall of Fame.

QUIZ ANSWER: The 1942 Toronto Maple Leafs, defeating the Detroit Red Wings

SEPTEMBER 11th

TODAY'S THOUGHT: "Be good or begone."
—*Bear Bryant*

HISTORY: On this date in 1985 Cincinnati's Pete Rose became Major League baseball's all-time hits leader, surpassing Ty Cobb's 4,191. When Rose retired, he left a new mark of 4,256 hits.

QUIZ: Who was the first woman to ride in the Kentucky Derby?

Trivia Timeout

In 1457 the Scottish Parliament banned the game of golf. The lawmakers felt that the time would be better spent practicing archery for defense against the English.

QUIZ ANSWER: Diane Crump, who finished 15th aboard Fathom in 1970

SEPTEMBER 12th

TODAY'S THOUGHT: "As I understand it, sport is hard work for which you do not get paid." —*Irvin S. Cobb*

HISTORY: On this date in 1976 Jimmy Connors defeated Bjorn Borg to win the second of his five U.S. Open titles.

QUIZ: Five players in Major League history have more than 3,000 hits and 400 home runs. How many do you recall?

Trivia Timeout

Despite playing in four U.S. Open finals, Bjorn Borg never won the tournament. Borg lost twice each to Jimmy Connors and John McEnroe.

QUIZ ANSWER: Stan Musial, Hank Aaron, Willie Mays, Carl Yastrzemski and Dave Winfield

SEPTEMBER 13th

TODAY'S THOUGHT: "Forget your opponents; always play against par." —*Sam Snead*

HISTORY: On this date in 1973 Congress passed legislation outlawing local TV blackouts of professional football games that are sold out three days in advance.

QUIZ: What Cuban-born player won batting titles in his first two years in the big leagues?

Trivia Timeout

Oakland A's slugger Mark McGwire, with 49 home runs and a chance to become the first Major League rookie to hit 50, passed up the final game of the 1987 campaign so he could be present at the birth of his son, Matthew.

QUIZ ANSWER: Tony Oliva of the Twins in 1964 and '65

SEPTEMBER 14th

TODAY'S THOUGHT: "Football is not a contact sport, it's a collision sport. Dancing is a good example of a contact sport." —*Duffy Daugherty*

HISTORY: On this date in 1923 Jack Dempsey knocked out Louis Firpo to retain his heavyweight title. Dempsey was knocked through the ropes and into the press row but, with the aid of sportswriters, was able to get back into the ring.

QUIZ: How many players are on each side in a Canadian Football League game?

Trivia Timeout

Sportscaster Brent Musburger was a baseball umpire in the Midwest League in 1959.

QUIZ ANSWER: 12

SEPTEMBER 15th

TODAY'S THOUGHT: "There are no points for style when it comes to putting. It's getting the ball to drop that counts." —*Brian Swarbrick*

HISTORY: On this date in 1969 Steve Carlton became the first pitcher in the 20th century to strike out 19 batters in a nine-inning game — but lost anyway. Carlton fanned everyone in the Mets lineup at least once, but Ron Swoboda hit two homers to defeat the Cardinals, 4-3.

QUIZ: What Celtics guard made the first NBA three-pointer?

Trivia Timeout

The original name suggested for basketball was "Naismith Ball" in honor of the game's inventor, James Naismith.

QUIZ ANSWER: Chris Ford

SEPTEMBER 16th

TODAY'S THOUGHT: "A school without football is in danger of deteriorating into a medieval study hall." —*Vince Lombardi*

HISTORY: On this date in 1975 Rennie Stennett led the Pirates to a 22-0 win over the Cubs, the most lopsided shutout in modern Major League history. Stennett sparked the club by going seven for seven.

QUIZ: In 1963 what native of New Zealand became the only left-handed golfer to win the British Open?

Trivia Timeout

The following night Stennett went three for five to set a modern record for most hits, 10, in two consecutive nine-inning games.

QUIZ ANSWER: Bob Charles

SEPTEMBER 17th

TODAY'S THOUGHT: "You never really lose until you stop trying." —*Mike Ditka*

HISTORY: On this date in 1963 the Houston Colt .45's started the first and only all-rookie lineup against Cincinnati. Despite Joe Morgan, Rusty Staub, Jim Wynn and Jerry Grote, Houston lost, 10-3.

QUIZ: In 1976 the NFL expanded by two teams. Who were these newcomers?

Trivia Timeout

Houston's rightfielder that day was a little-known player named Aaron Pointer. His better-known sisters had a few hits of their own — performing as the Pointer Sisters.

QUIZ ANSWER: The Seattle Seahawks and the Tampa Bay Buccaneers

SEPTEMBER 18th

TODAY'S THOUGHT: "The woods are full of long hitters." —*Harvey Penick*

HISTORY: On this date in 1968 Cardinals' pitcher Ray Washburn no-hit the Giants at Candlestick Park, 2-0. The day before Gaylord Perry of the Giants had no-hit St. Louis, 1-0.

QUIZ: True or false? While at Notre Dame Joe Theismann changed the pronunciation of his name from "THEEZ-man" to "THIGHS-man" to rhyme with Heisman—as in the trophy.

Trivia Timeout

Roger Maris hit only 275 career home runs.

QUIZ ANSWER: True, but the Heisman winner that year pronounced his name "PLUNKETT".

SEPTEMBER 19th

TODAY'S THOUGHT: "The man who complains about the way the ball bounces is likely the one who dropped it." —*Lou Holtz*

HISTORY: On this date in 1925 Bill Tilden became the first tennis player in this century to win six straight U.S. Opens. Tilden went on to win seven.

QUIZ: Mickey Mantle, Babe Ruth and Yogi Berra are the top three home run hitters in World Series history. What non-Yankee is fourth?

Trivia Timeout
The San Francisco Giants once had an outfield named "Alou". The three Alou brothers — Felipe, Jesus and Matty — played together in a game on September 15, 1963.

QUIZ ANSWER: Duke Snider of the Dodgers, with 11

SEPTEMBER 20th

TODAY'S THOUGHT: "Baseball is not precisely a team sport. It is more a series of concerts by the artists." —*Jim Murray*

HISTORY: On this date in 1987 Walter Payton broke Jim Brown's NFL record for rushing touchdowns with his 107th. Payton ended his career with 110.

QUIZ: Five Major Leaguers have won at least seven batting titles. How many can you remember?

Trivia Timeout
In his first NFL game, Walter Payton carried the ball eight times for a total of zero yards.

QUIZ ANSWER: Ty Cobb won 12 batting titles; Honus Wagner 8; Rod Carew 7; Rogers Hornsby 7; and Stan Musial 7.

SEPTEMBER 21st

TODAY'S THOUGHT: "When you're winning, you don't need any friends. When you're losing, you don't have any friends anyway." —*Woody Hayes*

HISTORY: On this date in 1985 Larry Holmes' bid to join Rocky Marciano as the only heavyweights to win 49 fights without a loss ended with a close decision for opponent Michael Spinks.

QUIZ: Coach John Wooden won his first NCAA basketball title in 1964. What team did his UCLA Bruins beat in the championship game?

Trivia Timeout

Michael Spinks is the only light heavyweight champ to successfully challenge for the heavyweight title.

QUIZ ANSWER: UCLA defeated Duke, 98-83.

SEPTEMBER 22nd

TODAY'S THOUGHT: "I would rather play Hamlet with no rehearsal than play golf on television."
—*Jack Lemmon*

HISTORY: On this date in 1911 the 22-year pitching career of Cy Young ended with victory number 511. Both Young's career wins and 750 complete games remain unchallenged as Major League records.

QUIZ: The son of what Cy Young Award winner in baseball has won more than a half million dollars on the PGA tour?

Trivia Timeout

Cy Young's real name is "Denton True Young".

QUIZ ANSWER: Jim Perry — His son is Chris Perry.

SEPTEMBER 23rd

TODAY'S THOUGHT: "The real superstar is a man or woman raising six kids on $150 a week."
—*Spencer Haywood*

HISTORY: On this date in 1957 Hank Aaron's 11th-inning home run powered the Braves past the Cardinals, 4-2, clinching the first Milwaukee pennant.

QUIZ: Two NBA players averaged more than 30 points per game in their rookie seasons. Who were they?

Trivia Timeout

Larry Bird has two streets named for him in Indiana: Larry Bird Avenue in Terre Haute, home of Indiana State, and Larry Bird Boulevard in French Lick, his hometown.

QUIZ ANSWER: Wilt Chamberlain averaged 37.6 points in 1959-60 and Oscar Robertson 30.5 in 1960-61.

SEPTEMBER 24th

TODAY'S THOUGHT: "Your body is just like a bar of soap. It gradually wears down from repeated use."
—*Richie Allen*

HISTORY: On this date in 1950 Chicago Cardinals quarterback Jim Hardy had a nightmarish day, throwing eight interceptions. Hardy redeemed himself the next week, however, with six TD passes.

QUIZ: Who was the oldest jockey to win the Kentucky Derby?

Trivia Timeout

The bottom of a tombstone in a Chicago area cemetery reads, in Yiddish, "The Cubs stink."

QUIZ ANSWER: Willie Shoemaker, riding Ferdinand, won in 1986 at age 54.

SEPTEMBER 25th

TODAY'S THOUGHT: "Sportswriting is the most pleasant way of making a living that man has yet devised." —*Red Smith, "New York Times" columnist*

HISTORY: On this date in 1988 the United States broke the world record in swimming's 400-meter medley relay at the Summer Olympics in Seoul.

QUIZ: Who was the youngest Major Leaguer to hit fifty home runs?

Trivia Timeout
Phil Rizzuto first tried out with the Dodgers where he was rebuffed by then Brooklyn manager Casey Stengel who told him, "Kid, you're too small...go out and shine shoes."

QUIZ ANSWER: Willie Mays, who hit 51 homers at age 24

SEPTEMBER 26th

TODAY'S THOUGHT: "Win and they carry you to the clubhouse on their shoulders; lose and you pay the caddies in the dark." —*Gene Sarazen*

HISTORY: On this date in 1983 the United States' domination of the America's Cup ended when the Australian challenger, *Australian II*, defeated the U.S. yacht, *Liberty*, four races to three. The United States had never lost the cup in the race's 132-year history.

QUIZ: True or false? At one time foul balls (except bunts or tips) were not counted as strikes.

Trivia Timeout
In 1968 former Dodger GM Al Campanis traded his son, Jim, to the Athletics for two minor leaguers.

QUIZ ANSWER: True, until the early 1900's

SEPTEMBER 27th

TODAY'S THOUGHT: "You're a fat football player, a fat baseball player, even a fat basketball player, a fat prizefighter, a fat golfer, lots of fat golfers, but never a fat tennis player." —*Jim Murray*

HISTORY: On this date in 1930 Bobby Jones won the U.S. Amateur, giving him a sweep of golf's major tournaments and the sport's Grand Slam.

QUIZ: This outfielder's eight seasons of 40 or more home runs are a Major League record. Who is it?

Trivia Timeout
Former heavyweight champion Leon Spinks was once mugged. The thugs made off with his money and jewelry — in addition to his two gold front teeth.

QUIZ ANSWER: Hank Aaron

SEPTEMBER 28th

TODAY'S THOUGHT: "Winning can be defined as the science of being totally prepared." —*George Allen*

HISTORY: On this date in 1969 quarterback Joe Kapp picked apart the Baltimore defense for 499 yards in the air, including seven touchdown passes, as Minnesota beat the Colts, 52-14. Eighteen years to the day earlier, Norm Van Brocklin threw for 554 yards, the NFL record.

QUIZ: The record for the most points in an NBA game is 370. Which teams reached this plateau?

Trivia Timeout
Pele perfected his game on the streets of Bauru, Brazil playing soccer with a bundle of rags wrapped in string.

QUIZ ANSWER: Detroit edged Denver, 186-184, in triple overtime.

SEPTEMBER 29th

TODAY'S THOUGHT: "If you don't have a hero, you'll never be disillusioned." —*Derek Sanderson*

HISTORY: On this date in 1987 Yankees first baseman Don Mattingly hit his sixth grand slam of the season, setting a new Major League record. The old mark had been shared by Ernie Banks and Jim Gentile.

QUIZ: How many time-outs is an NFL team allowed in a game?

Trivia Timeout
Before his record-breaking season, Mattingly had spent four years in the Majors without hitting a grand slam.

QUIZ ANSWER: Each team is allowed six time-outs, three in each half.

SEPTEMBER 30th

TODAY'S THOUGHT: "A true sports fan is one who can leave the game and ask, 'What cheerleaders?' "
—*Al Batt*

HISTORY: On this date in 1927 Babe Ruth became the first player to hit 60 home runs in one year.

QUIZ: Has any NBA player scored 4,000 points in a season?

Trivia Timeout
In a boxing match in 1923 Canadian flyweight champion Gene LaRue and challenger Kid Pancho simultaneously KO'd each other with haymaker lefts. The referee counted both fighters out.

QUIZ ANSWER: Yes, Wilt Chamberlain scored 4,029 points during the 1961-62 season.

OCTOBER 1st

TODAY'S THOUGHT: "There's nothing better in life than a head-on collision." —*Lawrence Taylor*

HISTORY: On this date in 1961 the Yankees' Roger Maris broke the record many thought never would be broken when he hit his 61st home run in the final game of season. Maris' blast off Tracy Stallard of the Red Sox bettered Babe Ruth's mark.

QUIZ: What NBA team did broadcaster Dick Vitale coach?

Trivia Timeout
Maris remains the only player to hit more than 50 home runs in a season yet bat less than .300. He hit .269 that record-breaking year.

QUIZ ANSWER: The Detroit Pistons, in 1978-79

OCTOBER 2nd

TODAY'S THOUGHT: "Golf is a puzzle without an answer." —*Gary Player*

HISTORY: On this date in 1968 Bob Gibson got St. Louis off to a good start in the first game of the World Series, striking out 17 Detroit batters in a 4-0 win.

QUIZ: Dan Marino was the sixth quarterback picked in the first round of the 1983 NFL draft. Name the other five.

Trivia Timeout
Until it officially opened in 1965, the Houston Astrodome was known as the Harris County Domed Stadium.

QUIZ ANSWER: John Elway (Colts), Todd Blackledge (Chiefs), Jim Kelly (Bills), Tony Eason (Patriots) and Ken O'Brien (Jets)

OCTOBER 3rd

TODAY'S THOUGHT: "Brooklyn is all right, but if you're not with the Giants, you might as well be in Albany." —*Bill Dahlen, Giants shortstop in 1904*

HISTORY: On this date in 1951 Bobby Thomson's three-run homer off Ralph Branca gave the New York Giants a 5-4 ninth-inning win over the Brooklyn Dodgers in game three of the NL playoffs — and the pennant. The blast was called "the shot heard 'round the world".

QUIZ: Who holds the record for the most PGA events won in one year?

Trivia Timeout
A home run by Thomson was also the margin of victory in the first playoff game that year. The pitcher? Ralph Branca.

QUIZ ANSWER: Byron Nelson, with 18 in 1945

OCTOBER 4th

TODAY'S THOUGHT: "It's almost like life. Just when it begins to look rosy, somebody will intercept a pass and run ninety yards against you."
—*John Facenda, NFL Films narrator*

HISTORY: On this date in 1895 Horace Rawlins shot rounds of 91 and 82 to capture golf's first U.S. Open, held in Newport, Rhode Island.

QUIZ: True or false? Gordon's Gin offers a one-million dollar reward to any person who can win two U.S. Opens.

Trivia Timeout
Benjamin Franklin, Julius Caesar and Winston Churchill are all members of the International Swimming Hall of Fame.

QUIZ ANSWER: True — with one hitch. The Opens must be in two different sports: golf and tennis.

OCTOBER 5th

TODAY'S THOUGHT: "College football today is one of the last great strongholds of genuine old-fashioned American hypocrisy." —*Paul Gallico*

HISTORY: On this date in 1985 Grambling's Eddie Robinson became college football's winningest coach, his 324 wins breaking the record held by Bear Bryant.

QUIZ: Besides the expansion teams of the nineties, only two Major League clubs have never had a pitcher throw a no-hitter. Name them.

Trivia Timeout
The 1992 Alabama football team had a freshman kicker whose name recalled a landmark Supreme Court decision, Wade Roe. His middle initial? V.

QUIZ ANSWER: The Mets and the Padres

OCTOBER 6th

TODAY'S THOUGHT: "Baseball has prostituted itself. Pretty soon we'll be starting games at midnight so people in outer space can watch on prime time television." —*Ray Kroc*

HISTORY: On this date in 1947 the Yankees defeated the Dodgers, 5-2, in the seventh game of the World Series. It also marked the first Series telecast.

QUIZ: Can you recall the last native of Great Britain to win the Men's Singles title at Wimbledon?

Trivia Timeout
Jockey Eddie Arcaro's career got out of the gate slowly. Arcaro won 4,779 races — but rode 250 losers before his first victory.

QUIZ ANSWER: Fred Perry, in 1935 and 1936

OCTOBER 7th

TODAY'S THOUGHT: "That is what this game is all about. If you can't play this game on emotion, don't show up." —*Mike Ditka, former Bears coach*

HISTORY: On this date in 1984 running back Walter Payton moved to the top of the list of the NFL's all-time leading rushers. Payton's 154-yard performance against the Saints gave him 12,400 career rushing yards, breaking the record held by Jim Brown.

QUIZ: Name the first tight end elected to the Pro Football Hall of Fame.

Trivia Timeout

Golfer Ben Crenshaw earned the nickname "Tarzan" by hitting so many drives into the woods.

QUIZ ANSWER: Mike Ditka, inducted in 1988

OCTOBER 8th

TODAY'S THOUGHT: "Ninety feet between home plate and first base may be the closest man has ever come to perfection." —*Red Smith*

HISTORY: On this date in 1956 Yankees pitcher Don Larsen hurled the only perfect game in World Series history, posting a 2-0 win over the Brooklyn Dodgers.

QUIZ: Who was the losing pitcher in Larsen's perfect game and who made the last out?

Trivia Timeout

Brooklyn shortstop Pee Wee Reese was the only batter to even reach ball three against Larsen. Reese was called out on strikes on a 3-2 pitch in the first inning.

QUIZ ANSWER: Sal Maglie and Dale Mitchell

OCTOBER 9th

TODAY'S THOUGHT: "You can shoot lions in the dark and yet you can quiver like a leaf and fall flat over a two-foot putt." —*Johnny Farrell*

HISTORY: On this date in 1916 the Red Sox' Babe Ruth showcased his talents in the World Series — as a pitcher. Ruth allowed just five hits over 13 innings in a 2-1 victory over the Dodgers.

QUIZ: Who is the only Major League pitcher with more than 100 career shutouts?

Trivia Timeout

Babe Ruth gave up only three runs as a pitcher in 31 World Series innings.

QUIZ ANSWER: Walter "Big Train" Johnson of the Washington Senators, with 110

OCTOBER 10th

TODAY'S THOUGHT: "There has never been a great athlete who died not knowing what pain is."
—*Bill Bradley*

HISTORY: On this date in 1987 Columbia University's football team set a record for futility when it lost its 35th game in a row. The Lion's 18-8 defeat by Princeton broke the mark set by Northwestern University.

QUIZ: In 1978 this Detroit Tiger became the first player to appear as a designated hitter in all 162 games. Who was it?

Trivia Timeout

Columbia snapped its losing streak at 44 the following season, beating Princeton, 16-14.

QUIZ ANSWER: Rusty Staub

OCTOBER 11th

TODAY'S THOUGHT: "Always remember — golf is like a beautiful woman. You can't take either for granted." —*Dan Valentine*

HISTORY: On this date in 1991 Chip Beck tied pro golf's all-time low score, shooting a 13-under-par 59 at the Las Vegas Invitational, matching Al Geiberger's 59 in the 1977 Memphis Classic.

QUIZ: In the 1957 Cotton Bowl, my Syracuse football team lost, 28-27, to TCU — despite my four touchdowns and three extra points. Who am I?

Trivia Timeout
Don Mattingly holds the season record for most at-bats without a stolen base: 677.

QUIZ ANSWER: Jimmy Brown

OCTOBER 12th

TODAY'S THOUGHT: "Games lubricate the body and the mind." —*Benjamin Franklin*

HISTORY: On this date in 1986 Dave Henderson stymied the Angels efforts to win their first pennant. The Red Sox outfielder hit a ninth-inning home run and an 11th-inning sacrifice fly to lead the Bosox to the AL championship.

QUIZ: Name the Heisman Trophy winner who also was a first-round NBA draft choice.

Trivia Timeout
The first woman in modern times to carry the Olympic torch was Norma Enriqueta Basilio Satelo in Mexico City in 1968.

QUIZ ANSWER: Quarterback Charlie Ward of Florida State was drafted as a guard by the Knicks.

OCTOBER 13th

TODAY'S THOUGHT: "It is committee meetings, called huddles, separated by outbursts of violence."
—*George Will, on football*

HISTORY: On this date in 1960 Bill Mazeroski's lead-off homer in the bottom of the ninth inning of game seven of the World Series gave the Pirates a 10-9 win over the Yankees. It was Pittsburgh's first Series championship in 35 years.

QUIZ: True or false? The 49ers' Jerry Rice has never led the NFL in scoring.

Trivia Timeout
Ralph Terry, the losing pitcher in that game, went on to play on the Senior PGA Tour.

QUIZ ANSWER: False. Rice led all scorers in 1987.

OCTOBER 14th

TODAY'S THOUGHT: "If a lot of people gripped a knife and fork like they do a golf club, they'd starve to death." —*Sam Snead*

HISTORY: On this date in 1964 unheralded Billy Mills became the first American to win the 10,000-meter run in the Summer Olympics.

QUIZ: Who is the only Major Leaguer in this century to get 200+ hits in seven consecutive seasons?

Trivia Timeout
John Wooden is the only man in the College Basketball Hall of Fame as a player and a coach. While best remembered for his tenure at UCLA, Wooden spent his playing days at Purdue.

QUIZ ANSWER: Wade Boggs, from 1983 to 1989

OCTOBER 15th

TODAY'S THOUGHT: "A little bit of perfume doesn't hurt you if you don't drink it."
—*Darrell Royal, former Texas football coach*

HISTORY: On this date in 1946 Enos Slaughter scored from first base on a double to provide the winning margin in St. Louis' seventh-game World Series win over Boston.

QUIZ: Since the 1969-70 season, the NBA has awarded its scoring title on the basis of per game average. Who was the first scoring leader under the new system?

Trivia Timeout

Enos Slaughter finished his 19-year Major League career with a batting average of exactly .300.

QUIZ ANSWER: Jerry West of the LA Lakers

OCTOBER 16th

TODAY'S THOUGHT: "It's a game in which you can feel a clean hatred for your opponent."
—*Ronald Reagan, on football*

HISTORY: On this date in 1969 the New York Mets completed their upset of Baltimore, downing the Orioles, 5-3, and becoming World Champions for the first time.

QUIZ: In 1979 I won the first sudden-death playoff in Masters history. Who am I?

Trivia Timeout

KEVIN McReynolds was traded from the Padres to the Mets in 1986 for KEVIN Mitchell, KEVIN Armstrong and KEVIN Brown.

QUIZ ANSWER: Fuzzy Zoeller

OCTOBER 17th

TODAY'S THOUGHT: "Like life, golf can be humbling. However, little good comes from brooding about mistakes we've made. The next shot, in golf or in life, is the big one." —*Grantland Rice*

HISTORY: On this date in 1860 Willie Park put together rounds of 55, 59 and 60 to win the first British Open.

QUIZ: Who holds the Major League record for RBI's in a season? Do you know how many?

Trivia Timeout
The first designated hitter to homer was the Twins' Tony Oliva.

QUIZ ANSWER: Hack Wilson of the Cubs, who knocked in 190 runs in 1930

OCTOBER 18th

TODAY'S THOUGHT: "In Czechoslovakia there (was) no such thing as freedom of the press. In the United States there is no such thing as freedom from the press." —*Martina Navratilova*

HISTORY: On this date in 1924 Red Grange dazzled Illinois football fans, running for four touchdowns in just six carries in the first quarter of a 39-14 win over Michigan.

QUIZ: Name the first U.S. club to join the NHL.

Trivia Timeout
Until 1857, when baseball adopted the nine innings per game rule, the first team to score 21 runs was declared the winner.

QUIZ ANSWER: The Boston Bruins, in 1924

OCTOBER 19th

TODAY'S THOUGHT: "Baseball is a ballet without music. Drama without words. A carnival without kewpie dolls." —*Ernie Harwell, broadcaster*

HISTORY: On this date in 1981 the Dodger's Rick Monday hit a ninth-inning home run to give LA a 2-1 victory over the Montreal Expos and the pennant.

QUIZ: Bear Bryant was head coach at four universities in his long career. His last two stops were Texas A&M and Alabama. What were the first two?

Trivia Timeout
Football great Sammy Baugh once threw four touchdown passes for the Washington Redskins and, playing defense, intercepted four Detroit Lions passes in the same game.

QUIZ ANSWER: Maryland and then Kentucky

OCTOBER 20th

TODAY'S THOUGHT: "This reporter from Fort Worth asked me, 'How much you think you'd be making now if you was playin'?' I said, 'Oh, about $500,000.' He said, 'Mick, guys are making $7 million a year now.' I said, 'Yeah, but I'm 60 years old.' "
—*Mickey Mantle, in 1992*

HISTORY: On this date in 1968 heavily-favored Jim Ryun was upset by Kip Keino of Kenya in the 1,500-meter race at the Olympics in Mexico City.

QUIZ: Can you name the only second baseman to hit 30 or more home runs in back-to-back seasons?

Trivia Timeout
Golfer Jack Nicklaus is color-blind.

QUIZ ANSWER: Ryne Sandberg in 1989 and 1990

OCTOBER 21st

TODAY'S THOUGHT: "Statistics always remind me of the fellow who drowned in a river whose average depth was only three feet." —*Woody Hayes*

HISTORY: On this date in 1980 the third time was the charm for the Philadelphia Phillies. After losing the World Series in 1915 and 1950, the Phils won their first championship, downing the Kansas City Royals.

QUIZ: Who was the last white boxer to wear the world heavyweight championship crown?

Trivia Timeout
New Orleans was awarded the Saint's NFL franchise on November 1, 1966. Coincidentally, November 1 is known as "All Saints Day".

QUIZ ANSWER: Ingemar Johansson, in 1959-60

OCTOBER 22nd

TODAY'S THOUGHT: "Look like a woman, but play like a man." —*Jan Stephenson, on golf*

HISTORY: On this date in 1950 the Rams lit up the scoreboard with a 70-27 trouncing of the Baltimore Colts. Los Angeles' high-powered offense unloaded again the next week, downing the Detroit Lions, 65-24.

QUIZ: With what team did Hall of Fame pitcher Robin Roberts finish his career?

Trivia Timeout
The 1950 Colts folded after one season in the NFL. A new Baltimore franchise, owned by Carroll Rosenbloom, began play in 1953.

QUIZ ANSWER: Roberts ended his career in 1966 with the Chicago Cubs.

OCTOBER 23rd

TODAY'S THOUGHT: "Our success doesn't come out of a computer. It comes out of the sweat glands of our coaches and players." —*Tom Landry*

HISTORY: On this date in 1964 Joe Frazier won the gold medal by decision in the Olympic heavyweight boxing finals in Tokyo. Frazier was a substitute for Buster Mathis who had broken a knuckle in training.

QUIZ: Doug Flutie received the Heisman Trophy in 1984. Who was the runner-up?

Trivia Timeout
After Frazier's bout, it was revealed that he had fought and won the gold with a broken right hand.

QUIZ ANSWER: Running back Keith Byars of Ohio State was runner-up.

OCTOBER 24th

TODAY'S THOUGHT: "Horses are like strawberries; you must enjoy them while you can, because they don't last long." —*Charlie Whittingham, trainer*

HISTORY: On this date in 1959 Wilt Chamberlain made his professional debut. The rookie center scored 43 points and pulled down 29 rebounds as his Philadelphia Warriors beat the New York Knicks, 118-109.

QUIZ: Can you name the five Major Leaguers with the most career hits?

Trivia Timeout
Y.A. Tittle's full name is "Yelberton Abraham Tittle".

QUIZ ANSWER: Pete Rose, Ty Cobb, Hank Aaron, Stan Musial and Tris Speaker are the top five.

OCTOBER 25th

TODAY'S THOUGHT: "I always wanted to be a player, but I never had the talent to make the big leagues. So I did the next best thing: I bought a team."
—*Charlie Finley*

HISTORY: On this date in 1986 an error by Bill Buckner in the 10th inning allowed the Mets to get by Boston, 6-5, forcing game seven in the World Series.

QUIZ: Two golfers with exactly three letters in their last names have won one of the major tournaments. Who?

Trivia Timeout
Cy Young is the only Major League pitcher to hurl no-hitters both before and after 1900.

QUIZ ANSWER: Ted Ray (1912 British Open and 1920 U.S. Open) and Ernie Els (1994 U.S. Open)

OCTOBER 26th

TODAY'S THOUGHT: "That little white ball won't move 'til you hit it, and there's nothing you can do after it's gone." —*Babe Didrikson Zaharias*

HISTORY: On this date in 1951 Joe Louis was knocked out by Rocky Marciano in the final fight of the "Brown Bomber's" career.

QUIZ: I coached my team to NBA titles in my last two years as a player. Who am I?

Trivia Timeout
Boxer Azumah Nelson was originally known as Nelson Azumah.

QUIZ ANSWER: Bill Russell of the Celtics who, as player coach, won the NBA championship in 1968 and '69

OCTOBER 27th

TODAY'S THOUGHT: "It's a very interesting game. They have big bears up front and little rabbits in the back. The idea is for the bears to protect the rabbits."
—*Viktor Tikonov, former Soviet hockey coach, on football*

HISTORY: On this date in 1991 the Minnesota Twins pushed across a run in the bottom of the tenth inning to beat Atlanta, 1-0, in game seven of the World Series.

QUIZ: What was the first NFL team to have two 1,000-yard rushers in one season?

Trivia Timeout
The Twins and Braves set a World Series record by playing three extra-inning games that year.

QUIZ ANSWER: The 1972 Miami Dolphins — Mercury Morris and Larry Csonka

OCTOBER 28th

TODAY'S THOUGHT: "If you aren't fired with enthusiasm, you'll be fired with enthusiasm."
—*Vince Lombardi*

HISTORY: On this date in 1962 Giants quarterback Y.A. Tittle threw seven touchdown passes in one game — only the fourth man to do so. His 505 passing yards sparked New York past Washington, 49-34.

QUIZ: Name the only father-son combination to hit home runs in the same inning for the same team.

Trivia Timeout
When Jack Norworth wrote the lyrics to "Take Me Out to the Ball Game" in 1908, he had never seen a Major League game.

QUIZ ANSWER: Ken Griffey, Sr. and Ken Griffey, Jr. hit back-to-back homers for the Seattle Mariners in 1990.

OCTOBER 29th

TODAY'S THOUGHT: "Baseball gives you every chance to be great. Then it puts every pressure on you to prove you haven't got what it takes." —*Joe Garagiola*

HISTORY: On this date in 1989 Tom Kite set a record for season's earnings with a sudden-death win in the Nabisco Championship. Kite finished the year with more than $1.3 million in winnings.

QUIZ: Which NBA team did Jerry Tarkanian coach?

Trivia Timeout

When National League umpire Tom Gorman died in 1986, he was buried in his blue umpire's suit, and with a ball and strike indicator in his hand. The count on it was 3-2.

QUIZ ANSWER: The San Antonio Spurs, for 20 games in 1992

OCTOBER 30th

TODAY'S THOUGHT: "It is almost impossible to remember how tragic a place the world is when one is playing golf." —*Robert Lynd*

HISTORY: On this date in 1973 Tom Seaver of the New York Mets became the first pitcher to win the Cy Young Award without amassing 20 victories. "Tom Terrific" was 19-10 with 18 complete games and a 2.08 ERA.

QUIZ: When Roger Maris belted 61 homers to lead the American League in 1961, who led the National League?

Trivia Timeout

Lou Gehrig's salary in 1927, as a member of the Yankee's "Murderer's Row", was $8,000.

QUIZ ANSWER: Orlando Cepeda of the San Francisco Giants with 46

OCTOBER 31st

TODAY'S THOUGHT: "If you can react the same way to winning and losing, that...quality is important because it stays with you the rest of your life." —*Chris Evert*

HISTORY: On this date in 1959 Oklahoma suffered its first and only conference defeat of the decade, losing to underdog Nebraska, 25-21.

QUIZ: Who was the last man to manage the Brooklyn Dodgers?

Trivia Timeout

Fenway Park in Boston has a secret message on its leftfield fence, the "Green Monster". The initials of the Red Sox late owners, Thomas and Jean Yawkey, are inscribed in Morse Code.

QUIZ ANSWER: Walter Alston, who retired in 1976

NOVEMBER 1st

TODAY'S THOUGHT: "It's not whether you win or lose, it's how you play the game." —*Grantland Rice*

HISTORY: On this date in 1964 Cleveland's Jim Brown ran for 149 yards against Pittsburgh to become the first NFL player to reach 10,000 career rushing yards. Meanwhile in the AFL, Houston's George Blanda was taking the high road — through the air — attempting a record 68 passes against Buffalo and completing 37.

QUIZ: In 1989 this man became the first draft pick ever for the Charlotte Hornets. Who was it?

Trivia Timeout

Sportswriter Grantland Rice gave fabled running back Red Grange his nickname, "The Galloping Ghost".

QUIZ ANSWER: North Carolina's J.R. Reid

NOVEMBER 2nd

TODAY'S THOUGHT: "My theory is that if you buy an ice-cream cone and make it hit your mouth, you can play. If you stick it on your forehead, your chances are less." —*Vic Braden, tennis instructor*

HISTORY: On this date in 1974 the Atlanta Braves traded Hank Aaron to the Milwaukee Brewers.

QUIZ: Name the three straight Heisman winners who, in the mid-80's, signed with the USFL instead of the NFL.

Trivia Timeout

The solid-bronze Heisman Trophy weighs 25 lbs.

QUIZ ANSWER: Herschel Walker ('82) signed with the New Jersey Generals, as did Doug Flutie ('84). Mike Rozier ('83) began his career with the Pittsburgh Maulers.

NOVEMBER 3rd

TODAY'S THOUGHT: "Our game plan is first year, a .500 season. Second year, a conference championship. Third year, undefeated. Fourth, a national championship. And by the fifth year, we'll be on probation, of course." —*Bear Bryant*

HISTORY: On this date in 1973 Brigham Young wide receiver Jay Miller set an NCAA record for receiving when he caught 22 passes in a game against New Mexico.

QUIZ: Who is the only Giant to win the Cy Young Award?

Trivia Timeout

When Bob Feller turned 22 in 1940, he already had won 82 Major League games.

QUIZ ANSWER: Mike McCormick won the award in 1967, going 22-10 with a 2.85 ERA.

NOVEMBER 4th

TODAY'S THOUGHT: "Golf is deceptively simple and endlessly complicated." —*Arnold Palmer*

HISTORY: On this date in 1979 the Rams held the Seahawks to minus-seven yards of total offense in a shutout win. Seattle quarterback Jim Zorn completed only two passes for one first down in the entire game.

QUIZ: "The outlook wasn't brilliant..." begins what famous poem?

Trivia Timeout

Father and son, Phil and Harold Johnson, were both KO'd by Jersey Joe Walcott — both in three rounds, both in Philadelphia, fourteen years apart.

QUIZ ANSWER: "Casey at the Bat"

NOVEMBER 5th

TODAY'S THOUGHT: "Tennis is a perfect combination of violent action taking place in an atmosphere of total tranquility." —*Billie Jean King*

HISTORY: On this date in 1971 the Lakers edged the Bullets, 110-106, starting a winning streak that didn't end until an NBA record 33 games and two months later.

QUIZ: Who was the first Major Leaguer to make the All-Star team as a catcher and then a second baseman?

Trivia Timeout
Basketball became an Olympic sport in 1936.

QUIZ ANSWER: Craig Biggio of the Houston Astros made the squad as a catcher in 1991 and then as a second baseman a year later.

NOVEMBER 6th

TODAY'S THOUGHT: "The invention of basketball was no accident...Those boys (at the Springfield, Massachusetts YMCA) simply would not play Drop the Handkerchief." —*Dr. James Naismith, inventor of basketball*

HISTORY: On this date in 1869 Rutgers and Princeton met in the first college football game. Rutgers won, 6-4.

QUIZ: True or false? Steffi Graf is the only woman to have won tennis' Grand Slam.

Trivia Timeout
James Naismith, founding father of the urban American sport of basketball, was born in rural Canada.

QUIZ ANSWER: False. Maureen Connolly (1953) and Margaret Court (1970) preceded Graf (1988) in winning tennis' four majors.

NOVEMBER 7th

TODAY'S THOUGHT: "Never have so many spent so much time to sit in relative comfort to brag about their failures." *—Keith Jackson, on golf*

HISTORY: On this date in 1963 Elston Howard was named Most Valuable Player in the American League. The Yankees catcher hit 28 homers and knocked in 85 runs on his way to being named the first black MVP in League history.

QUIZ: On this date in 1943 two teams played to the last scoreless tie in the NFL. Who were they?

Trivia Timeout

Elston Howard caught more World Series games than any other catcher — except fellow-Yankee Yogi Berra.

QUIZ ANSWER: The Giants and the Lions

NOVEMBER 8th

TODAY'S THOUGHT: "In this country when you finish second, no one knows your name." *—Frank McGuire*

HISTORY: On this date in 1970 Errol Mann's field goal gave Detroit a 17-16 lead over New Orleans with 11 seconds remaining in the game. But with two seconds left, Tom Dempsey kicked a record-breaking 63-yard field goal to give the Saints the win.

QUIZ: Name the first pitcher elected to the Baseball Hall of Fame with a losing record.

Trivia Timeout

Dempsey booted three other field goals that day totaling 64 yards — one yard more than the record-breaker alone.

QUIZ ANSWER: Satchel Paige, who was 28-31

NOVEMBER 9th

TODAY'S THOUGHT: "There are three important things in life: family, religion and the Green Bay Packers." —*Vince Lombardi*

HISTORY: On this date in 1989 the Milwaukee Bucks and Seattle Supersonics battled through five overtime periods. The Bucks perservered with a 155-154 victory.

QUIZ: Who replaced Lombardi as the Packers' coach?

Trivia Timeout

Bob Miller was a 6'1" right-handed pitcher for the 1962 New York Mets. Bob Miller was also a 6'1" left-handed pitcher for the 1962 Mets. No, Miller wasn't ambidextrous — there were two Bob Millers on the team.

QUIZ ANSWER: Phil Bengston

NOVEMBER 10th

TODAY'S THOUGHT: "You know horses are smarter than people. You never heard of a horse going broke betting on people." —*Will Rogers*

HISTORY: On this date in 1936 Eddie Arcaro was suspended for five months by the Maryland State Racing Commission for rough riding and fouling in a race at Pimlico.

QUIZ: Who holds the record for the most post-season appearances by a Major League baseball player?

Trivia Timeout

Gene Conley is the only athlete to play on world championship teams in both Major League Baseball and the NBA.

QUIZ ANSWER: "Mr. October" Reggie Jackson, with 77

NOVEMBER 11th

TODAY'S THOUGHT: "You can say something to popes, kings and presidents, but you can't talk to officials. In the next war, they ought to give everybody a whistle." —*Abe Lemons, basketball coach*

HISTORY: On this date in 1981 Fernando Valenzuela added the National League's Cy Young Award to his trophy collection. Valenzuela already had been named the League's Rookie of the Year.

QUIZ: True or false? Johnny Unitas and Dan Marino have the same middle name — Constantine.

Trivia Timeout

Valenzuela was the first player to win both awards in the same year.

QUIZ ANSWER: True

NOVEMBER 12th

TODAY'S THOUGHT: "When you land a good punch you can feel it in your arm, your hip, your shoulder, your toes, your toenails." —*Ken Norton*

HISTORY: On this date in 1920 Major League baseball's owners elected Judge Kenesaw Mountain Landis as the sport's first commissioner.

QUIZ: True or false? When Babe Ruth hit 54 home runs in 1920 and 60 in 1927, he had more homers than any other team in the American League those years.

Trivia Timeout

Max Baer, Jr., who played Jethro Clampett on television's "Beverly Hillbillies", is the son of the former heavyweight champion.

QUIZ ANSWER: True

NOVEMBER 13th

TODAY'S THOUGHT: "Testeverde looks like a quarterback, acts like a quarterback, he even talks like a quarterback. But he's got the heart of a placekicker." —*Tim McDonald, writer, on Vinny Testaverde*

HISTORY: On this date in 1939 the Board of Education in Coldwater, Michigan decreed that the Lincoln Rural School would be closed for deer hunting season, adding two weeks to the school year.

QUIZ: What movie featured Walter Matthau as the beer-drinking coach of a Little League team?

Trivia Timeout

The tackling dummy was invented by legendary football coach Amos Alonzo Stagg.

QUIZ ANSWER: "The Bad News Bears"

NOVEMBER 14th

TODAY'S THOUGHT: "He showed them it was a game, so they locked him up." —*Abbie Hoffman, on Jimmy Piersall, who was once committed to a mental hospital*

HISTORY: On this date in 1943 Sid Luckman became the first NFL quarterback to toss seven touchdown passes, as the Chicago Bears crushed the New York Giants, 56-7.

QUIZ: Who is the National League career leader in grand slams?

Trivia Timeout

Jimmy Piersall's troubled life warranted its own movie, "Fear Strikes Out". The lead was played by actor Anthony Perkins — better known for his role as Norman Bates in "Psycho".

QUIZ ANSWER: Willie McCovey, with 18

NOVEMBER 15th

TODAY'S THOUGHT: "By the time you get dressed, drive out there, play 18 holes, and come home, you've blown seven hours. There are better things you can do with your time." —*Richard Nixon*

HISTORY: On this date in 1960 Lakers forward Elgin Baylor put on a scoring exhibition, tallying 71 points in a 123-106 win over the Knicks.

QUIZ: Who was the first college football player to gain more than 6,000 yards rushing?

Trivia Timeout

Baylor remains one of only four NBA players to score 70 or more points in a game. Wilt Chamberlain did it six times; David Robinson and David Thompson each did it once.

QUIZ ANSWER: Pitt's Tony Dorsett, from 1973-76

NOVEMBER 16th

TODAY'S THOUGHT: "I read over the years that I was as much a Bay Area landmark as the Golden Gate Bridge. But I'm going and that bridge isn't going anywhere." —*Nate Thurmond, after being traded from the Warriors to the Bulls*

HISTORY: On this date in 1957 college football's longest winning streak came to an end as Notre Dame upset Oklahoma, 7-0. The Sooners had won 47 straight games.

QUIZ: Which NBA team was the only expansion club to qualify for the playoffs in its first season?

Trivia Timeout

Before that shutout, Oklahoma had scored in 123 consecutive games.

QUIZ ANSWER: The 1966-67 Chicago Bulls

NOVEMBER 17th

TODAY'S THOUGHT: "When I was in high school, I was called a hothead when I lost my temper. When I got in the Major Leagues, they called me a competitor." —*Billy Martin*

HISTORY: On this date in 1968 NBC cut away from the Raiders-Jets football game to show the movie "Heidi". Angry fans missed seeing Oakland score two touchdowns in nine seconds to beat New York, 43-32.

QUIZ: Who was the first baseball player to have his uniform number retired?

Trivia Timeout

The odds of a major-college football or basketball player making the pros are 100:1.

QUIZ ANSWER: Lou Gehrig

NOVEMBER 18th

TODAY'S THOUGHT: "Nothing goes down slower than a golf handicap." —*Bobby Nichols*

HISTORY: On this date in 1954 the Orioles and Yankees stoked the hot stove with a monumental 17-player trade that featured—among others—Bob Turley and Don Larsen.

QUIZ: True or false? An NFL player once scored 40 points in a single game.

Trivia Timeout

India withdrew from the 1950 World Cup when soccer's governing body wouldn't allow its team to play barefoot.

QUIZ ANSWER: True. In 1929 Ernie Nevers propelled the Chicago Cardinals past the Bears, 40-6, with six touchdowns and four extra points.

NOVEMBER 19th

TODAY'S THOUGHT: "I never want to quit playing ball. They'll have to cut this uniform off me to get me out of it." —*Roy Campanella*

HISTORY: On this date in 1966 Notre Dame and Michigan State squared off in a battle of college football's two top-ranked teams, fighting to a 10-10 tie. Both schools finished the season with 9-0-1 records, but the Irish were declared national champs.

QUIZ: Which two sets of brothers have hit homers as Major League teammates in the same inning?

Trivia Timeout

The maximum allowable weight for a golf ball is 1.62 oz.

QUIZ ANSWER: Cal and Billy Ripken for the Orioles, and Paul and Lloyd Waner for the Pirates

NOVEMBER 20th

TODAY'S THOUGHT: "When you're playing for the national championship, it's not a matter of life or death. It's more important than that." —*Duffy Daugherty*

HISTORY: On this date in 1977 Walter Payton set a new single-game rushing record. Payton busted loose for 275 yards in the Bears 10-7 win over the Vikings.

QUIZ: What player became center for the UCLA basketball team when Kareem Abdul-Jabbar graduated in 1969?

Trivia Timeout

Payton ground out his final 65 yards that day with less than three minutes left in the game.

QUIZ ANSWER: Steve Patterson was thrust into the starter's role.

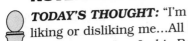

NOVEMBER 21st

TODAY'S THOUGHT: "I'm not concerned with your liking or disliking me...All I ask is you respect me as a human being." —*Jackie Robinson*

HISTORY: On this date in 1971 the New York Rangers scored eight third-period goals on their way to a 12-1 victory over the California Golden Seals. The record held up for almost a decade.

QUIZ: This man is the only person to coach in the NFL championship game six years in a row. Who is he?

Trivia Timeout

Stan Musial was the first inductee into the Polish-American Sports Hall of Fame and Museum.

QUIZ ANSWER: Paul Brown led the Cleveland Browns to title games from 1950 to 1955, winning three.

NOVEMBER 22nd

TODAY'S THOUGHT: "The sad fact is that it looks more and more as if our national sport is not playing at all — but watching." —*John F. Kennedy*

HISTORY: On this date in 1986 Mike Tyson became the youngest man to win a heavyweight title. The 20-year old boxer knocked out Trevor Berbick in the second round to capture the WBC crown.

QUIZ: Name the only second baseman in Major League history to win back-to-back MVP awards.

Trivia Timeout

"Yankee Clipper" Joe DiMaggio played in every inning of every All-Star Game from 1936 through 1942.

QUIZ ANSWER: Joe Morgan of the Cincinnati Reds earned the MVP in 1975 and '76.

NOVEMBER 23rd

TODAY'S THOUGHT: "Prayer never seems to work for me on the golf course. I think it has something to do with my being a terrible putter." —*Reverend Billy Graham*

HISTORY: On this date in 1984 Doug Flutie's "Hail Mary" pass with six seconds left in the game fell into the hands of receiver Gerald Phelan to give Boston College a dramatic 47-45 win over Miami.

QUIZ: Who was the first center to lead the NBA in scoring and rebounding in the same season?

Trivia Timeout

Flutie was the first quarterback to throw for 10,000 yards in his college career.

QUIZ ANSWER: Neil Johnston of the Philadelphia Warriors did it during the 1954-55 season.

NOVEMBER 24th

TODAY'S THOUGHT: "Quick guys get tired. Big guys don't shrink." —*Marv Harshman, Washington Huskies basketball coach on speed vs. size*

HISTORY: On this date in 1960 Wilt Chamberlain pulled down a record 55 rebounds in a 132-129 loss to the Celtics. The Warriors center topped the mark of 51 set by the man defending him that night, Bill Russell.

QUIZ: Who holds the NFL record for the most interceptions in a season?

Trivia Timeout

Rogers Hornsby is big league baseball's only .400/40 man. The former Cardinal hit .401 and slugged 42 homers in 1922.

QUIZ ANSWER: Dick "Night Train" Lane intercepted 14 passes in 1952 for the Los Angeles Rams.

NOVEMBER 25th

TODAY'S THOUGHT: "I'm a ballplayer, not an actor."
—*Joe DiMaggio, on his on-field decorum*

HISTORY: On this date in 1941 the Cleveland Indians named 24-year old shortstop Lou Boudreau player-manager. Boudreau is the last player-manager to triumph in the World Series.

QUIZ: What slugger has hit the most home runs in a single Major League park — and where?

Trivia Timeout
New York Yankees outfielder Gene Woodling homered off Early Wynn of the Cleveland Indians on June 24, July 24 and August 24, 1951.

QUIZ ANSWER: Mel Ott of the New York Giants, with 323 four-baggers in the Polo Grounds

NOVEMBER 26th

TODAY'S THOUGHT: "I signed a contract, and I pitch for what I signed for. Think about it — your signature on a contract is the same as your word."
—*Nolan Ryan, explaining a pay cut*

HISTORY: On this date in 1956 Bob Richards of the U.S. won his second straight Olympic gold medal in the pole vault. Richards cleared the bar at 14' 11-1/2" in the Summer Games in Melbourne, Australia.

QUIZ: Who was the first Major Leaguer to be named Rookie of the Year and MVP in the same season?

Trivia Timeout
Nike is the Greek goddess of victory.

QUIZ ANSWER: Fred Lynn of the Boston Red Sox took both awards in 1975.

NOVEMBER 27th

TODAY'S THOUGHT: "Tackling is more natural than blocking. If a man is running down the street with everything you own, you won't let him get away. That's tackling." —*Vince Lombardi*

HISTORY: On this date in 1966 the defense rested. The Redskins outscored the Giants, 72-41, breaking the old mark of 70 points set by the Rams in 1950.

QUIZ: Name the infielder who played in all 44 Yankee-Brooklyn Dodger World Series games.

Trivia Timeout

The opposing place-kickers were the Gogolak brothers. Charlie had a field goal and nine extra points for Washington, while Pete converted after five of the New York TD's.

QUIZ ANSWER: Shortstop Pee Wee Reese of the Dodgers

NOVEMBER 28th

TODAY'S THOUGHT: "On Thanksgiving Day all over America, families sit down to dinner at the same moment — halftime." —*Anonymous*

HISTORY: On this date in 1979 Billy Smith of the Islanders became the first NHL goalie to be credited with a goal after an opposing player accidentally shot the puck into his own net.

QUIZ: True or false? Cooperstown, New York, the home of the Baseball Hall of Fame, was named for the father of novelist James Fenimore Cooper.

Trivia Timeout

During the Korean War the Cincinnati Reds changed their name to the Redlegs for political reasons.

QUIZ ANSWER: True

NOVEMBER 29th

TODAY'S THOUGHT: "I don't think we can win every game. Just the next one." —*Lou Holtz*

HISTORY: On this date in 1976 the Yankees signed free-agent outfielder Reggie Jackson to a five-year contract. New York won three American League pennants and two World Series with Jackson.

QUIZ: I caught 12 passes in the 1958 NFL Championship and later coached in the Super Bowl. Who am I?

Trivia Timeout
The St. Louis "Post-Dispatch" once featured this golf headline: "Shot off Woman's Leg Helps Nicklaus to 66".

QUIZ ANSWER: Raymond Berry, who played with the Colts in '58 and took the New England Patriots to Super Bowl XX

NOVEMBER 30th

TODAY'S THOUGHT: "When people tell me I could be the best athlete there is, I just let it go in one ear and out the other. There is always somebody out there who is better than you are. Go ask Mike Tyson." —*Bo Jackson*

HISTORY: On this date in 1990 Larry Bird of the Boston Celtics joined the 20,000 point club, the 15th NBA player to reach this plateau.

QUIZ: How many Major League players have hit 600 or more career home runs?

Trivia Timeout
The New York Knickerbockers became the first pro baseball club to wear hats — straw hats — in 1852.

QUIZ ANSWER: Three — Hank Aaron (755), Babe Ruth (714) and Willie Mays (660)

DECEMBER 1st

TODAY'S THOUGHT: "I ask them to give us a lot of money, but not their two cents." —*Joe Paterno, on alumni*

HISTORY: On this date in 1956 the United States basketball team, led by Bill Russell and K.C. Jones, won the gold medal at the Summer Olympics in Melbourne, downing the Soviets, 89-55.

QUIZ: Can you name the only player to win the Heisman Trophy despite playing on a team with a losing record?

Trivia Timeout
In earlier times, the Indianapolis 500 and other auto races had two people riding in the car: a driver and a mechanic.

QUIZ ANSWER: Paul Hornung won the Heisman in 1956, when Notre Dame finished the season at 2-8.

DECEMBER 2nd

TODAY'S THOUGHT: "One year I hit .291 and had to take a salary cut. If you hit .291 today, you own the franchise." —*Enos Slaughter*

HISTORY: On this date in 1972 Anthony Davis ran roughshod over Notre Dame, scoring six touchdowns in USC's 45-23 win.

QUIZ: Only one Kansas City Royals player has ever been named Rookie of the Year. Who?

Trivia Timeout
Raiders cornerback Willie Brown set an NFL record by intercepting at least one pass each season during his 16-year career.

QUIZ ANSWER: Outfielder Lou Piniella won the honor in 1969, the franchise's first year.

DECEMBER 3rd

TODAY'S THOUGHT: "(Auto) racing is 99 percent boredom and one percent terror." —*Geoff Brabhan*

HISTORY: On this date in 1966 sophomore center Lew Alcindor gave UCLA basketball fans an idea of what was to come. Playing in his first game for the Bruins, Alcindor scored 56 points in a win over USC.

QUIZ: Name the winning and losing pitchers in the 1978 AL playoff between the Yankees and Red Sox.

Trivia Timeout

At a 1990 New York City auction, a Shoeless Joe Jackson autograph was sold for $23,100, the most ever paid for the signature of a 19th or 20th century famous figure.

QUIZ ANSWER: Ron Guidry got the win over Mike Torrez to capture the AL East.

DECEMBER 4th

TODAY'S THOUGHT: "If you don't get it by midnight, chances are you ain't gonna get it, and if you do it ain't worth it." —*Casey Stengel*

HISTORY: On this date in 1977 the Tampa Bay Buccaneers walked the plank to their 26th consecutive loss. The expansion franchise's first win ever came the following week against New Orleans.

QUIZ: The University of Cincinnati won the NCAA basketball championship in 1961 and '62. It beat the same team in the finals both times. Name the school.

Trivia Timeout

Elston Howard invented the "donut" used by on-deck hitters.

QUIZ ANSWER: The Bearcats beat Ohio State, 70-65, in overtime in 1961 and then 71-59, in 1962.

DECEMBER 5th

TODAY'S THOUGHT: "Even Betty Crocker burns a cake now and then." —*Bill Caudell, relief pitcher, on "off" days*

HISTORY: On this date in 1984 Helena Sukova ended Martina Navratilova's 74-match winning streak. Sukova won, 1-6, 7-3, 7-5, in the semifinals of the Australian Open.

QUIZ: Name the only Major Leaguer to knock in more than 100 runs in a season after reaching his 40th birthday.

Trivia Timeout

The real name of boxing great Willie Pep is Guglielmo Papaleo.

QUIZ ANSWER: Dave Winfield had 108 RBI's at the age of 40 for the Toronto Blue Jays in 1992.

DECEMBER 6th

TODAY'S THOUGHT: "Prizefighting offers a profession to men who otherwise might commit murder in the street." —*Heywood Hale Broun*

HISTORY: On this date in 1921 Cleveland Browns quarterback legend Otto Graham was born.

QUIZ: I won the heavyweight title in 1962, knocking out the champ in two minutes, six seconds of the first round. Ten months later, I KO'd the same man at two minutes, 10 seconds of the first round. Who am I?

Trivia Timeout

Hank Aaron and Babe Ruth were both members of the Braves when they hit home run number 714.

QUIZ ANSWER: Sonny Liston was the victor; Floyd Patterson was the victim.

DECEMBER 7th

TODAY'S THOUGHT: "I really don't like talking about money. All I can say is that the Good Lord must have wanted me to have it." —*Larry Bird*

HISTORY: On this date in 1963 CBS introduced instant replay during the Army-Navy game.

QUIZ: Two college basketball players have led the nation in scoring three consecutive years. Name them.

Trivia Timeout
Former baseball player Carlos May is the only big leaguer to have worn his birthday on his back. His number was 18 and his last name, which appeared above the number, combined with it to form his birth date.

QUIZ ANSWER: Cincinnati's Oscar Robertson from 1958-60 and LSU's Pete Maravich from 1968-70

DECEMBER 8th

TODAY'S THOUGHT: "A lot of guys who have never choked, have never been in the position to do so."
—*Tom Watson*

HISTORY: On this date in 1940 Chicago crushed Washington, 73-0, in the most lopsided NFL championship game ever.

QUIZ: Lawrence Taylor was the second player taken in the 1981 NFL draft. Who was chosen first?

Trivia Timeout
That game marked the first national radio broadcast of an NFL title game. The Mutual Broadcasting System paid $2,500 for the rights.

QUIZ ANSWER: The New Orleans Saints passed on "LT" and took Heisman Trophy winner George Rogers.

DECEMBER 9th

TODAY'S THOUGHT: "When we played, World Series checks meant something. Now all they do is screw up your taxes." —*Don Drysdale*

HISTORY: On this date in 1984 the Rams' Eric Dickerson gained 216 yards on the ground against the Houston Oilers to eclipse the NFL's single-season rushing record. Dickerson's big day brought his total to 2,007 yards, four more than O.J. Simpson had accumulated eleven years earlier.

QUIZ: On what three continents did Muhammad Ali win his four heavyweight titles?

Trivia Timeout
The most common nickname in baseball history is "Lefty".

QUIZ ANSWER: North America, Africa and Asia

DECEMBER 10th

TODAY'S THOUGHT: "You know if you kill somebody they sentence you to life, you serve twenty years and you get paroled. I've never been paroled."
—*Ralph Branca, on the notoriety from giving up Bobby Thomson's "shot heard 'round the world"*

HISTORY: On this date in 1971 the Mets traded pitcher Nolan Ryan and three other players to the California Angels for shortstop Jim Fregosi.

QUIZ: How many Super Bowls have gone into OT?

Trivia Timeout
The 1944 World Series was played by teams from the same city and the same park. The St. Louis Browns faced the St. Louis Cardinals at Sportsman's Park.

QUIZ ANSWER: 0

DECEMBER 11th

TODAY'S THOUGHT: "Because there is always some kid who may be seeing me for the first or last time."
—*Joe DiMaggio, on why he played so hard*

HISTORY: On this date in 1951 Joe DiMaggio announced his retirement from baseball.

QUIZ: In 1993 these two Major Leaguers hit 46 home runs apiece to lead their respective leagues. Name them.

Trivia Timeout

Carlos Baerga of the Cleveland Indians is the only player to hit a right-handed homer and a left-handed homer in the same inning. He did so in the seventh inning of a game against the New York Yankees on April 7, 1993.

QUIZ ANSWER: Juan Gonzalez of the Texas Rangers and Barry Bonds of the San Francisco Giants

DECEMBER 12th

TODAY'S THOUGHT: "When God rang the bell and ended the fight, the world cried out for one round more." —*Jesse Jackson, eulogizing Sugar Ray Robinson*

HISTORY: On this date in 1965 two of the NFL's legendary running backs combined for eleven touchdowns. Paul Hornung scored five TD's while Gale Sayers tallied six.

QUIZ: Who holds the Major League record for most consecutive innings played?

Trivia Timeout

St. Louis Hawks forward Bob Pettit was the first NBA player to score 20,000 points.

QUIZ ANSWER: Cal Ripken, Jr., with 8,243, from June 5, 1982 to September 14, 1987

DECEMBER 13th

TODAY'S THOUGHT: "It's funny...you need a fantastic memory in this game to remember the great shots and a very short memory to forget the bad ones."
—*Gary McCord, on golf*

HISTORY: On this date in 1960 Italy downed the U.S. in international Davis Cup competition marking the first time in 24 years that the American team had failed to make the finals.

QUIZ: In 1992 what player became the first since Babe Ruth to lead the AL in RBI's for three straight years?

Trivia Timeout
The Washington Redskins were the Boston Redskins before moving to D.C. in 1937.

QUIZ ANSWER: Cecil Fielder of the Detroit Tigers

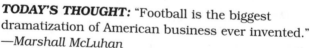

DECEMBER 14th

TODAY'S THOUGHT: "Football is the biggest dramatization of American business ever invented."
—*Marshall McLuhan*

HISTORY: On this date in 1988 the expansion Miami Heat enjoyed the thrill of victory for the first time after experiencing the agony of defeat in 17 straight games.

QUIZ: Where did the Montreal Expos play before moving to Olympic Stadium?

Trivia Timeout
Bad news/good news: Danny London, a popular deaf-mute boxer, lost a fight in 1929 after taking a ferocious punch to the head. The good news was, after he regained his senses, he found that he could hear and speak once again.

QUIZ ANSWER: Jarry Park

The Bathroom Sports Almanac

DECEMBER 15th

TODAY'S THOUGHT: "The arc of your swing doesn't have a thing to do with the size of your heart."
—Carol Mann, on golf

HISTORY: On this date in 1980 the Yankees signed outfielder Dave Winfield to the most lucrative contract in sports, a reported $25 million deal.

QUIZ: Only two freshmen have been named Most Outstanding Player in the NCAA basketball tournament. Arnie Ferrin of Utah was honored in 1944. Who was the other player?

Trivia Timeout
Roger Maris holds the national high school record for most TD's scored on kick-off returns in a single game—four.

QUIZ ANSWER: Pervis Ellison of Louisville, in 1986

DECEMBER 16th

TODAY'S THOUGHT: "Statistics are like a bikini; they show a lot but not everything." *—Lou Piniella*

HISTORY: On this date in 1962 Y.A. Tittle tossed six touchdown passes in the Giants 41-31 win over Dallas, setting a new NFL season record of 33.

QUIZ: What quarterback currently holds the single-season record for passing touchdowns?

Trivia Timeout
In Ron Guidry's 25-3 season in 1978, all three losses by the Yankee hurler were to a pitcher named "Mike": Mike Caldwell, Mike Flanagan and Mike Willis.

QUIZ ANSWER: Dan Marino of the Miami Dolphins completed 48 TD tosses in 1984.

DECEMBER 17th

TODAY'S THOUGHT: "The key is to concentrate through bad times." —*Dan Fouts, former NFL quarterback*

HISTORY: On this date in 1933 the NFL held its first championship game at Chicago's Wrigley Field. The Bears, led by Bronko Nagurski, edged the New York Giants, 23-21.

QUIZ: In 1957 North Carolina won two straight triple-overtime games on its way to the NCAA basketball championship. One victory was against Kansas in the final. Who was the victim in the semi-final contest?

Trivia Timeout

Football historians claim the quarterback's exclamation of "hut" for the snap stems from Army drill sergeants.

QUIZ ANSWER: The Tarheels beat Michigan State.

DECEMBER 18th

TODAY'S THOUGHT: "The great trouble with baseball today is that most of the players are in the game for the money that's in it — not for the love of it, the excitement of it, the thrill of it." —*Ty Cobb, in 1925*

HISTORY: On this date in 1930 Adolph Rupp began his 41-year basketball coaching career at Kentucky, dumping Georgetown, 67-19.

QUIZ: Do you recall the uniform number of Walter Payton, the NFL's all-time leading rusher?

Trivia Timeout

Adolph Rupp's teams captured four NCAA championships and one NIT for Kentucky.

QUIZ ANSWER: Payton wore number 34, which has been retired by the Bears.

DECEMBER 19th

TODAY'S THOUGHT: "He never lost a game in his life. Once in a while time ran out on him." —*Doak Walker, former Detroit Lion, on teammate Bobby Layne*

HISTORY: On this date in 1984 the Buffalo Sabres beat the Chicago Blackhawks, 6-3, making Scotty Bowman the NHL's all-time winningest coach with 691 victories.

QUIZ: The NFL record for sacks in a season is 22. Who set this mark?

Trivia Timeout
Ken "Hawk" Harrelson, who played pro golf as well as in the Major Leagues, was the first baseball player to wear a batting glove.

QUIZ ANSWER: Mark Gastineau, while playing for the Jets in 1984

DECEMBER 20th

TODAY'S THOUGHT: "The greatest untapped reservoir of raw material in the history of our game is the black race." —*Branch Rickey, after signing Jackie Robinson*

HISTORY: On this date in 1980 NBC broadcast the game between the Jets and Dolphins without announcers. Viewers were aided by graphics and the stadium's public address system in this one-time experiment. By the way, the Jets won, 24-17.

QUIZ: What two Yankees have led the American League in homers since Roger Maris hit his 61 in '61?

Trivia Timeout
"Nahgroodnick" is Russian for baseball's chest protector.

QUIZ ANSWER: Graig Nettles, with 32 in 1976 and Reggie Jackson, who tied for the lead with 41 in 1980

DECEMBER 21st

TODAY'S THOUGHT: "The minute you think you've got it made, disaster is just around the corner."
—*Joe Paterno*

HISTORY: On this date in 1981 Doug Schloemer's shot with one second left ended college basketball's longest game. The basket gave Cincinnati a 75-73 win over Bradley in the seventh overtime period.

QUIZ: In the NFL, which referee is responsible for timing the game?

Trivia Timeout
Tennis great Jimmy Connors was dubbed "le Grognon" by the French — or "the Grunter".

QUIZ ANSWER: The line judge

DECEMBER 22nd

TODAY'S THOUGHT: "   " —*Steve Carlton, to the media*

HISTORY: On this date in 1969 LSU's Pete Maravich set an NCAA record when he sank 30 of 31 free throws against Oregon State.

QUIZ: Troy Aikman's pass hits a referee and bounces away. Emmitt Smith catches the ball before it hits the ground and runs for a touchdown. Does the TD count?

Trivia Timeout
Oakland A's reliever Darold Knowles is the only man to have pitched in each game of a seven-game World Series. Knowles' name appeared in every box score in Oakland's Series triumph over the New York Mets in 1973.

QUIZ ANSWER: Yes

DECEMBER 23rd

TODAY'S THOUGHT: "Experience is the name we give our mistakes."
—*Fred Shero, former New York Rangers coach*

HISTORY: On this date in 1972 Franco Harris made the "Immaculate Reception" that put the Steelers in the AFC Championship game.

QUIZ: In baseball circles, Morganna King is better known by what nickname?

Trivia Timeout
Connie Mack's real name is Cornelius McGillicuddy.

QUIZ ANSWER: The Kissing Bandit

DECEMBER 24th

TODAY'S THOUGHT: "Why am I wasting so much dedication on a mediocre career?" —*Ron Swoboda*

HISTORY: On this date in 1982 tiny Chaminade College pulled off one of basketball's biggest upsets. The Silverswords outdueled the top-ranked Virginia Cavaliers, 77-72, limiting All-American center Ralph Sampson to 12 points.

QUIZ: Who was the first National League player to win back-to-back Most Valuable Player awards?

Trivia Timeout
Sampson and Chaminade center Tony Randolph had faced each other previously in high school in Virginia.

QUIZ ANSWER: Cubs shortstop Ernie Banks turned this MVP double play.

DECEMBER 25th

TODAY'S THOUGHT: "The perfect Christmas gift for a sportscaster, as all fans of sports cliches know, is a scoreless tie." —*William Safire*

HISTORY: On this date in 1971 Miami and Kansas City played the NFL's longest game. The outcome wasn't decided until the Dolphins' Garo Yepremian kicked a 37-yard field goal more than 22 minutes into overtime. Miami advanced in the playoffs with the 27-24 win.

QUIZ: Who was the only NBA coach to win Coach of the Year honors twice during the 80's?

Trivia Timeout
The game was the grand finale for KC's Municipal Stadium.

QUIZ ANSWER: Don Nelson, of the Milwaukee Bucks in 1983 and '85

DECEMBER 26th

TODAY'S THOUGHT: "Golf is wonderful exercise. You can stand on your feet for hours, watching someone else putt." —*Will Rogers*

HISTORY: On this date in 1960 Chuck Bednarik stopped Jim Taylor on the 10-yard line as time expired in the NFL championship game. Bednarik's tackle preserved the Eagles' 17-13 win over the Green Bay Packers.

QUIZ: What golf course has Amen Corner?

Trivia Timeout
Par represents the number of strokes an expert golfer should need on a given hole.

QUIZ ANSWER: Augusta National Golf Course

DECEMBER 27th

TODAY'S THOUGHT: "The toughest hole is the 19th."
—*Craig Stadler*

HISTORY: On this date in 1992 Packers wide receiver Sterling Sharpe made six catches to raise his season total to 108 and break Art Monk's NFL season mark of 106.

QUIZ: Three men have led the NBA in assists at least six times each. Name them.

Trivia Timeout

The actual playing time in a 2-1/2 hour baseball game has been clocked at 9 minutes, 55 seconds.

QUIZ ANSWER: Bob Cousy, Oscar Robertson and John Stockton

DECEMBER 28th

TODAY'S THOUGHT: "Knowin' all about baseball is about as profitable as bein' a good whittler." —*Abe Martin*

HISTORY: On this date in 1958 the NFL championship was decided by sudden death for the first time. Alan Ameche's touchdown run after eight minutes of overtime gave the Colts a 23-17 win over the Giants.

QUIZ: Who was the first manager to win a pennant in both the National and American Leagues?

Trivia Timeout

"Arena" football pre-dates the NFL. The first indoor pro football game was played in 1902 in New York's Madison Square Garden, as Syracuse downed Philadelphia, 6-0.

QUIZ ANSWER: Joe McCarthy, with the Cubs in 1929 and the Yankees in 1932

DECEMBER 29th

TODAY'S THOUGHT: "Quit coaching? I'd croak in a week." —*Bear Bryant, who died of a heart attack a month after retiring*

HISTORY: On this date in 1978 Ohio State lost the Gator Bowl and their head coach. After a Clemson interception, Buckeyes coach Woody Hayes erupted and punched the Tiger player who picked off the ball. Hayes was relieved of his duties by the university.

QUIZ: What was the name of the Clemson player whose interception enraged Woody Hayes and cost him his job?

Trivia Timeout
The National Negro Baseball League was formed in 1920.

QUIZ ANSWER: Charlie Bauman

DECEMBER 30th

TODAY'S THOUGHT: "In one day I went from a negative presence to a man with a great past."
—*Jim Palmer, on retiring*

HISTORY: On this date in 1990 Orlando guard Scott Skiles dished out 30 assists to set an NBA record.

QUIZ: True or false? Richie Ashburn won more National League batting titles than Willie Mays.

Trivia Timeout
Phil Wrigley would have installed lights at Wrigley Field as early as 1942 had it not been for World War II. The Chicago Cubs owner purchased the lights but decided to donate them to a shipyard to aid the war effort instead.

QUIZ ANSWER: True. Ashburn was the NL batting champ in 1955 and '58. Mays won the title once, in 1954.

DECEMBER 31st

TODAY'S THOUGHT: "It ain't over till it's over."
—*Yogi Berra*

HISTORY: On this date in 1967 Bart Starr's one-yard plunge with 13 seconds remaining gave the Packers a 21-17 win over the Dallas Cowboys and their third straight NFL title. Over 50,000 fans braved below-zero temperatures at Green Bay's Lambeau Field.

QUIZ: The movie "Raging Bull" portrayed what boxer?

Trivia Timeout

In 1931 Cleveland Indians' catcher Joe Sprinz caught a baseball dropped 800 feet from a balloon. The impact created such a jolt through his body that it broke his jaw.

QUIZ ANSWER: Jake LaMotta, played by Robert DeNiro in an Oscar-winning performance